Nelson MATHEMATICS 5

towards LEVEL 5 and Beyond

PUPILS' BOOK 1

Nelson

Thomas Nelson and Sons Ltd
Nelson House Mayfield Road
Walton-on-Thames Surrey
KT12 5PL UK

51 York Place
Edinburgh
EH1 3JD UK

Thomas Nelson (Hong Kong) Ltd
Toppan Building 10/F
22A Westlands Road
Quarry Bay Hong Kong

Thomas Nelson Australia
102 Dodds Street
South Melbourne
Victoria 3205
Australia

Nelson Canada
1120 Birchmount Road
Scarborough Ontario
M1K 5G4 Canada

Authors and consultants
Bill Domoney
Peter Gash
Paul Harrison
Lorely James
David Kirkby
Ann Sawyer
Diana Wright

Contributors
Paul Broadbent
Brenda Stevens

Acknowledgements

Photography
Allsport: page 47; Chris Ridgers: pages 6, 8, 29, 36 (no. 7),
39, 40, 41, 57, 93, 120; Zefa: pages 36 (except no. 7), 115.

The authors and publishers would like to thank British
Rail and the National Westminster Bank for the use of
their logos on page 29.

Design
Julia King, Thumbnail Graphics

Illustration
Jane Cheswright
Karen Donnelly
Jackie East
Peter Kent
Stan Stevens
Nancy Sutcliffe
Charles Whelon

Produced by **AMR**

First published by Thomas Nelson & Sons Ltd 1993

ISBN 0-17-421632-7 (single copies)
ISBN 0-17-421633-5 (pack of 6)
NPN 9 8 7 6 5 4 3 2 1

Printed in Hong Kong

CONTENTS

The colour band at the foot of each page indicates the relevant section of the **Teacher's Resource File, Level 5 and Beyond**.

Order of operations

Remember: in an expression with several operations:
First do the operations in Brackets.
Second do any Divisions.
Then any Multiplications.
Finally do any Additions and Subtractions.
An easy way to remember this is BoDMAS.
(The 'o' stands for 'of'.)

Several children were asked to find the value of:

$48 \div 6 + 2 \times 5 - 4$

They gave 5 different answers:

6, 46, 10, 26, 14

1. Which answer is correct?

In these expressions brackets have been used
to help make the order clear.

What is the value of:

2. $(4 \times 8) - (6 \div 2) \times 5$

3. $(9 - 5) + (4 \times 8) - (15 \div 15)$

4. $16 - (9 \times 4) \div 36$

5. $4 \times (24 \div 6) - 10 + 5$

6. $9 \times 12 \times 2 \div 12$

Make them true

Copy these expressions and put in the brackets
to make them true statements.

1. $5 \times 7 - 3 = 20$

2. $28 - 13 - 6 = 21$

3. $6 - 5 \times 12 = 12$

4. $38 - 23 + 17 - 12 = 10$

5. $48 \div 12 + 6 \times 6 = 1$

6. $23 - 18 - 5 \times 7 = 0$

7. $5 \times 6 \div 13 - 10 = 10$

8. $8 \times 7 - 2 = 40$

Remember: > means 'is greater than'
< means 'is less than'
= means 'is equivalent to'

Copy these, then use $<$, $>$ or $=$ to make true statements.

9. $(8 + 7) \times 5$? $8 + 7 \times 5$

10. $7 + 2 \times 4$? $5 \times 2 + 6$

11. $5 \times 9 \div 3$? $8 + 4 \times 8$

12. $23 - 12 \div 6$? $2 + 6 \times 3$

13. $5 \times 5 \div 5$? $5 \div 5 \times 5$

14. $36 \div 12 \div 3$? $24 \div 12 \div 2$

There is more about brackets on page 44.

Very big numbers

Kilowatt hours (kW h)

thousands   hundreds   tens   ones

> Ten 100 W (watt) light bulbs left on for 1 h (hour) use 1 kW h of energy.

The dials show the number of kilowatt hours of electrical energy used.

$$(2 \times 1000) + (5 \times 100) + (6 \times 10) + (7 \times 1) = 2567$$

expanded form   **ordinary form**

A place value chart helps us to read large numbers.

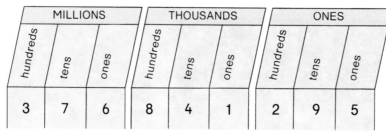

| MILLIONS | | | THOUSANDS | | | ONES | | |
hundreds	tens	ones	hundreds	tens	ones	hundreds	tens	ones
3	7	6	8	4	1	2	9	5

376 841 295 is read '376 million 841 thousand 295'.

The 3 in 376 841 295 has a value of 3 hundred million.

Write these meter readings in ordinary form and expanded form.

1.

2.

Words and numbers

Use your calculator to work out the answers to these.
Write the answers in words.

1.   sixty thousand plus seven thousand plus five hundred

2.   eight hundred thousand subtract fifty thousand

3.   seven hundred plus eight plus thirty thousand plus four thousand

4.   sixty-eight thousand one hundred subtract thirty thousand five hundred and forty

5.   eight hundred and five thousand and twenty plus six million one hundred and ninety thousand three hundred and ten

---

6. **Where does it end?**

Take any 4 digits. **3 1 2 6**

Make the largest number possible. **6 3 2 1**

Subtract the smallest number possible. **1 2 3 6**

The answer is: **5 0 8 5**

Now do the same with the digits 5085.

Do the same with each resulting number to make a number chain.

Where does this chain end?

Investigate this for other sets of 4 digits.

What do you notice?

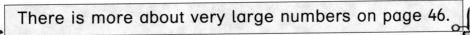

There is more about very large numbers on page 46.

Ways of finding factors

Remember: the factors of a number can be multiplied to make that number. For example, the factors of 6 are 1, 2, 3 and 6 (because 1 x 6 = 6 and 2 x 3 = 6).

Miss Masters has 24 children in her PE lesson.

She uses factors of 24 to group them for different exercises.

Here is an organised method for finding all the factors of 24.

Try 1:   1 x 24 = 24   1 and 24 are factors of 24.

Try 2:   2 x 12 = 24   2 and 12 are factors of 24.

Try 3:   3 x 8 = 24   3 and 8 are factors of 24.

Try 4:   4 x 6 = 24   4 and 6 are factors of 24.

Try 5:   5 x ? = 24   5 is not a factor of 24.

Try 6:   6 is already known to be a factor of 24.

The factors of 24 are 1, 2, 3, 4, 6, 8, 12 and 24.

---

1. On squared paper, draw all the possible rectangles that can be made from 36 squares.

2. There will be 40 guests at a dinner. All the tables must have the same number of people at them. What are the possible seating arrangements.

3. a. What is the area of the front of this envelope?

    b. Find all the possible dimensions for envelopes with the same area.

    c. Which of these are practical for envelopes?

9cm

20cm

Fun with factors

6 is a perfect number.

The factors of 6, apart from 6 itself, are 1, 2 and 3.

Because 1, 2 and 3 add up to 6, we call 6 a perfect number.

1. There is another perfect number between 10 and 30.
    Find it and explain how it is perfect.

2. There is another between 490 and 500.
    Try to find this one.

12 is an abundant number.

The factors of 12, apart from 12 itself, are 1, 2, 3, 4 and 6.

These factors add up to more than 12, so we call 12 an abundant number.

10 is a deficient number.

The factors of 10, apart from 10 itself, are 1, 2 and 5.

These add up to less than 10, so 10 is called a deficient number.

3. Which numbers between 2 and 20 are abundant?

4. Which numbers between 90 and 100 are deficient?

There is more about factors on page 48.

Positive and negative numbers

The blue car is 3 levels above the ground level. This can be shown as +3.

   positive three

+3 is a positive number.

+1, +2, +3 +4 ... are positive numbers. (They can also be shown as 1, 2, 3, 4 ...)

The yellow car is 3 levels below the ground level. This can be shown as −3.

   negative three

−3 is a negative number.

−1, −2, −3, −4 ... are negative numbers. (The negative sign is always shown.)

0 is neither positive nor negative.

Above and below are opposites.
+3 and −3 are opposites.

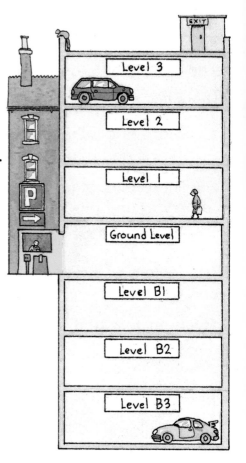

Which sign would you use for these?

1. 7°C below freezing point.

2. 6 floors above ground level.

3. 50 m below sea level.

4. I owe 25p.

5. You are 6 steps in front of me.

6. Nick Faldo was 4 under par.

7. £300 over the estimate.

8. The cook was 8 school dinners short.

Savings accounts

This is a page from Yasmin's bank book.

Date	Pay in	Withdraw	Balance
14.3.93	Cash 5.00		5.00
21.3.93	Cash 1.50		6.50
24.3.93	Cash	−2.00	4.50
1.4.93	Cheque 10.00		
1.4.93	Cash	−5.00	9.50
4.4.93	Cash	−1.50	
11.4.93	Cheque	−5.00	

The balance is how much there is in the account.
Paying money in increases the balance.
Taking money out decreases the balance.

1. When did Yasmin open the account?

2. What was the balance on 5th April 1993?

3. What was the balance after she took out a cheque?

4. How much did she put into the account in the period shown?

5. How much did she take out of the account in the period shown?

Three decimal places

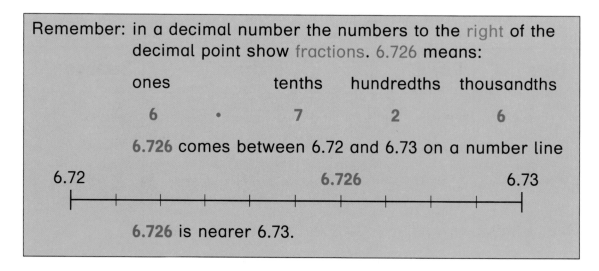

Remember: in a decimal number the numbers to the right of the decimal point show fractions. 6.726 means:

ones		tenths	hundredths	thousandths
6	.	7	2	6

6.726 comes between 6.72 and 6.73 on a number line

6.72   6.726   6.73

6.726 is nearer 6.73.

Draw number lines to show these decimals.
Say which number with 2 decimal places
they are nearer to.

1.	3.127	2.	10.862	3.	23.524
4.	9.511	5.	16.968	6.	10.729
7.	5.026	8.	4.244	9.	15.967

Make up some similar problems for a friend.

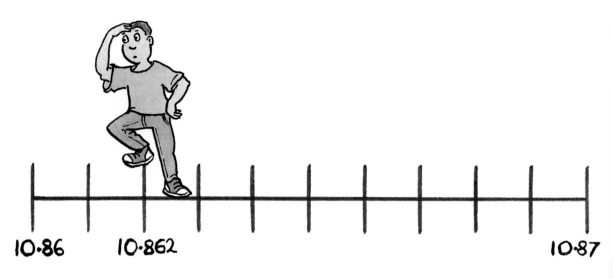

10·86   10·862   10·87

Rounding decimals

Remember: when rounding a decimal you look at the last digit.

If the digit is less than 5 the decimal rounds down: 1.642 rounds down to 1.64.

If the digit is more than 5, or 5 itself, the decimal rounds up: 1.647 rounds up to 1.65, and 1.645 rounds up to 1.65.

Round these decimals up or down to 2 decimal places.

1. 23.534   2. 8.609   3. 0.815   4. 15.033

5. 19.965   6. 0.083   7. 5.728   8. 1.232

Round these to the nearest whole number.

9. 8.475   10. 3.125   11. 6.666

12. 0.561   13. 10.328   14. 2.725

15.   Is your height nearer to 1 m or 2 m?

There is more about decimals on page 52.

Converting fractions to decimals

> Remember: in order to convert a fraction to a decimal, divide the
> numerator by the denominator. For example,
>
> $\frac{1}{4}$ is $1 \div 4 = .25$

Use a calculator to divide the numerator by the denominator to
convert these fractions to decimals. Where the answer is not exact,
give it correct to 2 decimal places.

1. $\frac{1}{2}$
2. $\frac{1}{5}$
3. $\frac{1}{3}$
4. $\frac{1}{8}$

Now do the same with these fractions.

5. $\frac{3}{5}$
6. $\frac{4}{10}$
7. $\frac{2}{9}$
8. $\frac{5}{6}$

With mixed numbers you only need to change the fractional part.
For example,

$2\frac{1}{4} = 2.25$

Try the same method with these mixed numbers:

9. $4\frac{4}{5}$
10. $6\frac{1}{4}$
11. $8\frac{3}{10}$
12. $3\frac{5}{8}$

Write out some different fractions for a friend to
convert to decimals.

Fractions between

If you draw a number line like this, you can see that the number halfway between $\frac{3}{4}$ and $1\frac{3}{4}$ is $1\frac{1}{4}$.

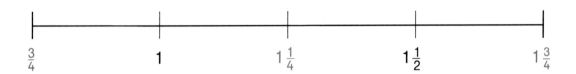

$\frac{3}{4}$ 1 $1\frac{1}{4}$ $1\frac{1}{2}$ $1\frac{3}{4}$

Write the fraction or decimal halfway between these numbers.
You may wish to draw another number line.
You may need to convert between fractions and decimals.

1. $\frac{2}{10}$ and $\frac{8}{10}$

2. .25 and $\frac{3}{4}$

3. 1.3 and $2\frac{3}{10}$

4. $\frac{3}{5}$ and $\frac{4}{5}$

5. 0.5 and 0.75

6. 2.75 and 3

7. 5.3 and 5.6

8. 6.1 and 6.2

9. $\frac{1}{2}$ and 0.8

10. 10.25 and $10\frac{1}{2}$

11. Name a number between $\frac{3}{10}$ and $\frac{2}{5}$.

12. Name 3 numbers between 2.5 and $2\frac{7}{8}$.

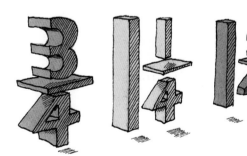

There is more about fractions on page 54.

Writing ratios

Here is 1 red cube and
3 blue cubes.

We say 'The ratio of red to
blue is one to three'.
We write it 1:3.

Here are 2 yellow cubes and
8 green cubes.

The ratio of green to yellow is 8:2,
which is the same as 4:1.

Sometimes a ratio will not have 1 in it.
These cubes are 3:2, orange to black.

Write the ratio of red to blue for these pictures.

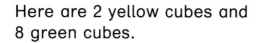

1.

2.

3.

4.

5.

6.

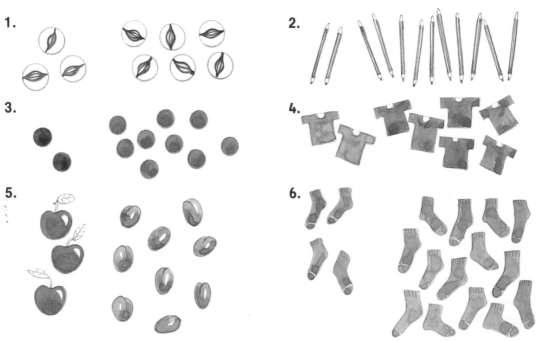

Birdwatching

In an hour, these birds visited a garden.

4 blackbirds

6 thrushes

12 starlings

24 sparrows

2 blue tits

1 wagtail

Write down the ratio of:

1. starlings to blackbirds

2. bluetits to starlings

3. thrushes to starlings

4. sparrows to each of the other birds

In a survey of water birds these were the ratios.

Mallards to geese 6:1

Mallards to teal 5:2

5. If there were 30 mallards, how many geese and teal were there?

6. If 12 mallards flew away, what would the new ratios be?

There is more about ratio on page 56.

How many diagonals?

It is impossible to draw a diagonal from one vertex of
a triangle to another.

In any quadrilateral it is possible to draw a diagonal from
one vertex to another.

Number of sides	Number of diagonals from one vertex
3	0
4	1
5	
6	

1. Carry on with the chart. Try 5, 6, 7 and 8-sided shapes
   (regular and irregular).

2. How many diagonals could you draw from one vertex
   of a 20-sided shape?

3. How could you work out the number of diagonals from
   one vertex of any shape?

4. Now investigate the total number of diagonals in
   3, 4, 5, 6, 7 and 8-sided shapes. Describe any
   patterns you find.

Matchstick patterns

This is a pattern of squares formed by matchsticks.

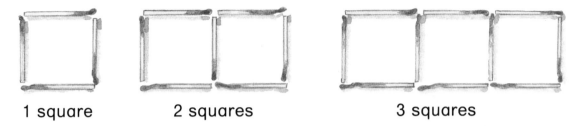

1 square   2 squares   3 squares

1. How would you make the next in the sequence?

2. Copy and continue this chart until you can see a
   pattern in the number of matchsticks.
   Describe the pattern.

Position	Number of squares	Number of matchsticks
1	1	4
2	2	7
3	3	10
4		

3. How many matchsticks are needed for the 100th
   position in the sequence?

4. How could you work out the number of matchsticks
   for any position in the sequence?

Handshakes

Investigate how many times a group of people need
to shake hands when they meet for the first time.

If 2 people meet, they only
need to shake hands once.

If 3 people meet, there will be
3 handshakes.

1. If 4 people meet, how many
    handshakes will there be?

2. Carry on investigating with different numbers of people.
    Make a table on squared paper to record your results.

Number of people	1	2	3	4	5	6	7
Number of handshakes	0	1	3				

3. Describe how the pattern grows. Try to find a quick
    way of working out how many handshakes there
    would be between 100 people.

Squares on a chessboard

How many squares can you see in this 2 x 2 grid?

There are 5,

4 small (1 x 1) squares

and 1 large (2 x 2) one.

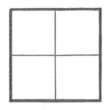

1. How many squares are there in a 3 x 3 grid?

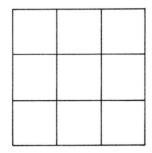

2. Try the next in the series (4 x 4).

Make a chart to show the number of squares you can see.

Grid size	1 x 1 squares	2 x 2 squares	3 x 3 squares	4 x 4 squares	5 x 5 squares	Total
1 x 1	1					1
2 x 2	4	1				5
3 x 3	9	4	1			

3. Now predict how many squares on a 5 x 5 grid? Check by counting.

4. Describe any patterns you see.

5. Use pattern to work out how many squares on an 8 x 8 chessboard.

There is more about patterns on page 58.

Use the formula

Remember: the area of a rectangle is the surface it covers. The area can be found by multiplying the length by the breadth.

$l \times b = a$

$4 \text{ cm} \times 2 \text{ cm} = 8 \text{ cm}$

breadth 2 cm

length 4 cm

We say: Length x breadth is the **formula** for area.

The perimeter is the distance all the way around a shape. The perimeter can be found by multiplying the length and breadth by 2.

(Length + breadth) x 2 is the **formula** for perimeter.

Here is a chart of dimensions for some rectangles. Copy it and fill in the missing information.

length 4 cm

breadth 2 cm

$2 \times (l + b) = p$

$2 \times (4 \text{ cm} + 2 \text{ cm})$
$= 12 \text{ cm}$

	length	breadth	area	perimeter
1.	5 cm	3 cm		
2.		2 cm		16 cm
3.	9 cm		36 cm^2	
4.		8 cm		36 cm
5.	7 cm			24 cm
6.	15 cm		90 cm^2	
7.		6 cm	72 cm^2	
8.		4 cm		24 cm

9. Find some rectangles in the classroom.
   Measure them and find their areas and perimeters.

There is more about areas on page 60.

Another formula

This circle has been drawn on graph paper to show its area. It has 4 cm^2 and 8 other squares which are almost 1 cm^2. This is approximately 12 cm^2. There are also 4 smaller parts of squares. We can say its area is 'a bit more than 12 cm^2'.

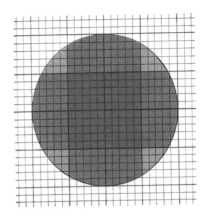

There is a formula for the area of a circle:

Area $= \pi \times \text{radius}^2$

π (pronounced like 'pie') is a letter in the Greek alphabet.

It is used to represent a special number: 3.14 (correct to 2 decimal places).

So for the circle shown: Area $= 3.14 \times 2^2 = 3.14 \times 4 = 12.56 \text{ cm}^2$.

Find the areas of these circles by drawing them on graph paper and counting big and small squares. Check by using the formula $A = \pi \times r^2$.

1. radius 5 cm
2. radius 8 cm
3. radius 6 cm
4. radius 3 cm

5. Copy and complete this chart.

π	r	r^2	area
3.14	9 cm		
3.14		49 cm^2	
3.14			50.24 cm^2

There is more about circles on page 61.

9-pin areas

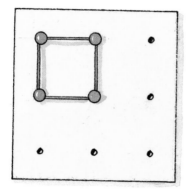

This square has an area of 1 unit.

What are the areas of these quadrilaterals (4-sided shapes)?

1.

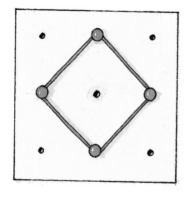

2.

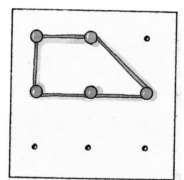

3.

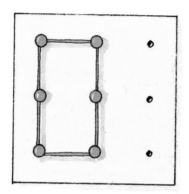

4.

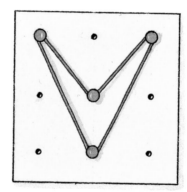

Make some more quadrilaterals on a 9-pin geoboard.
Work out their areas.

Dissecting parallelograms

You can make rectangles from parallelograms
by cutting and rearranging.

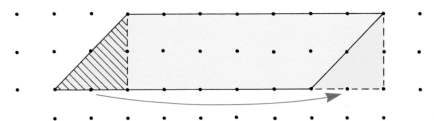

Copy or trace these parallelograms and cut them,
rearranging to make rectangles.

Write down their areas.

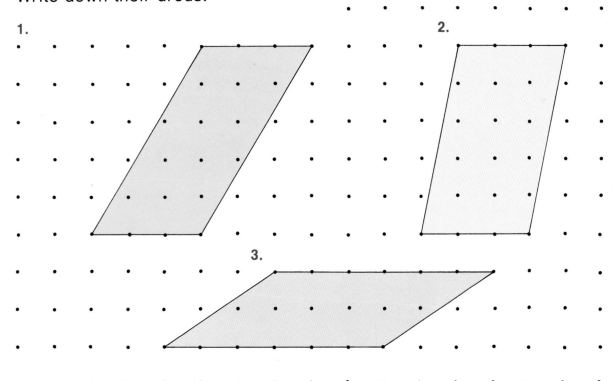

1.

2.

3.

4. If you know the length of the base and the height of
    a parallelogram, how can you work out its area?

There is more about areas of parallelograms on page 65.

Check your image

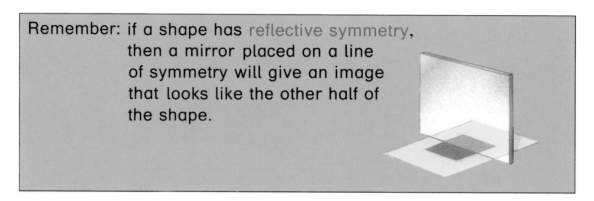

Remember: if a shape has reflective symmetry, then a mirror placed on a line of symmetry will give an image that looks like the other half of the shape.

Trace or sketch these shapes and draw any lines of symmetry in different colours.

You can check with a mirror. If your line of symmetry is correct, you will see the other half of the shape in the mirror.

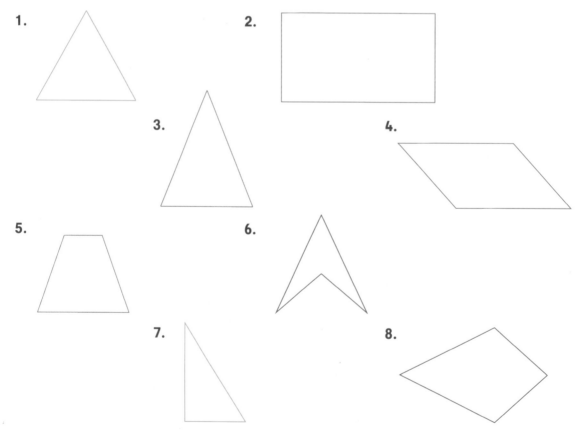

1.

2.

3.

4.

5.

6.

7.

8.

Cutting solids

The grapefruit has symmetry because both halves are identical (congruent).

If a sheet of clear acetate is placed between the two halves as shown, the acetate becomes the plane of symmetry.

A plane of symmetry divides a solid shape into identical halves in the same way that a line of symmetry divides a plane flat shape.

State the number of planes of symmetry.

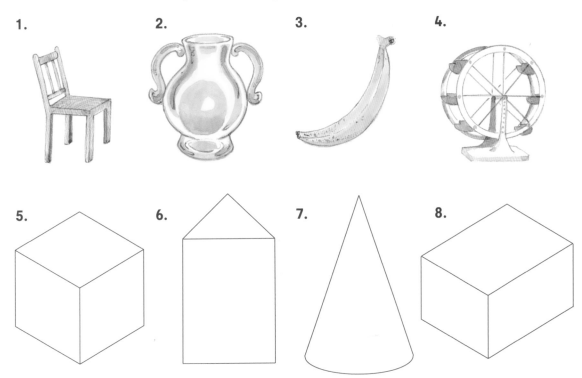

1.

2.

3.

4.

5.

6.

7.

8.

9. List 3 things in your classroom that have no planes of symmetry.

10. List 3 things in your classroom that have more than one plane of symmetry.

Rotational symmetry

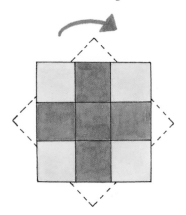

If this pattern is rotated it will fit into its outline 4 times. We say the pattern has rotational symmetry of order 4.

This pattern also has reflective symmetry. It has 4 lines of symmetry.

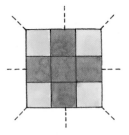

1. What order of rotational symmetry does this pattern have?

2. Does it have reflective symmetry?

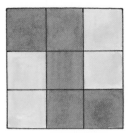

3. What order of rotational symmetry does this pattern have?

4. How many lines of symmetry does it have?

5. Colour 5 squares to make a pattern with reflective symmetry but **no** rotational symmetry.

Investigate other patterns for rotational and reflective symmetry.

Spinning logos

Many common shapes and patterns have rotational symmetry. What order of symmetry do these have?

1.

2.

Logos are designed to look good.
What order of rotational symmetry do these have?

3.

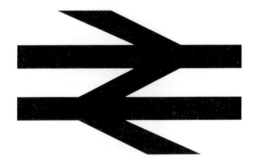

4.

5.

6. Design a logo for your class. Decide what order of rotational symmetry it should have.

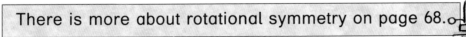

There is more about rotational symmetry on page 68.

Goblin caves

The x and y axis drawn on the map can be used to describe a position. The distance along the x axis is written first. This is called the x co-ordinate. The distance up or down the y axis is the y co-ordinate.

On the plan of the Goblin caves the x co-ordinate of Short Dead End is −2, the y co-ordinate is 5. The co-ordinates are written (−2, 5).

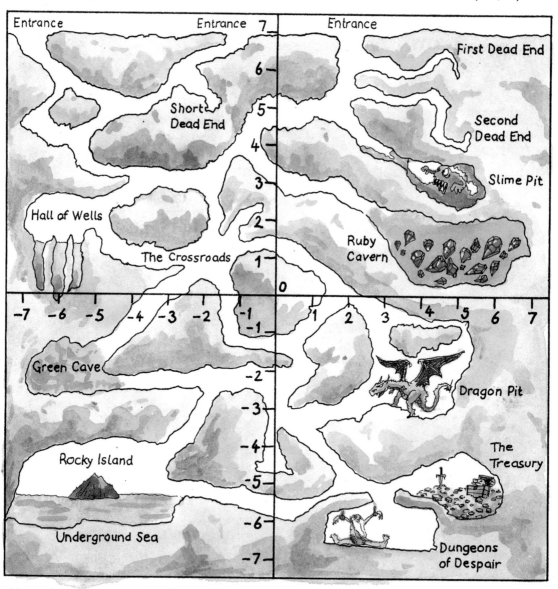

Use the plan of the Goblin caves to answer the questions on page 31.

Location and transformation of shapes   Unit 1   Four quadrant co-ordinate map

Places in the goblin caves

What would you find at:

1. (−6, 2)

2. (5, 4)

3. Whose entrance is at (3, 2)?

4. What hazard is at (4, −2)?

5. What is unpleasant at (5, 3)?

Write the co-ordinates for:

6. The Entrances.

7. The Green Cave.

8. The Rocky Island.

9. The Crossroads.

10. The Dungeons of Despair.

Design your own map or plan. Use co-ordinates to describe some positions on your map.

There is more about co-ordinates on page 70.

Radar map

This is a radar map of a busy seaway.
The rings are 1 mile apart. The rays are 10° apart.

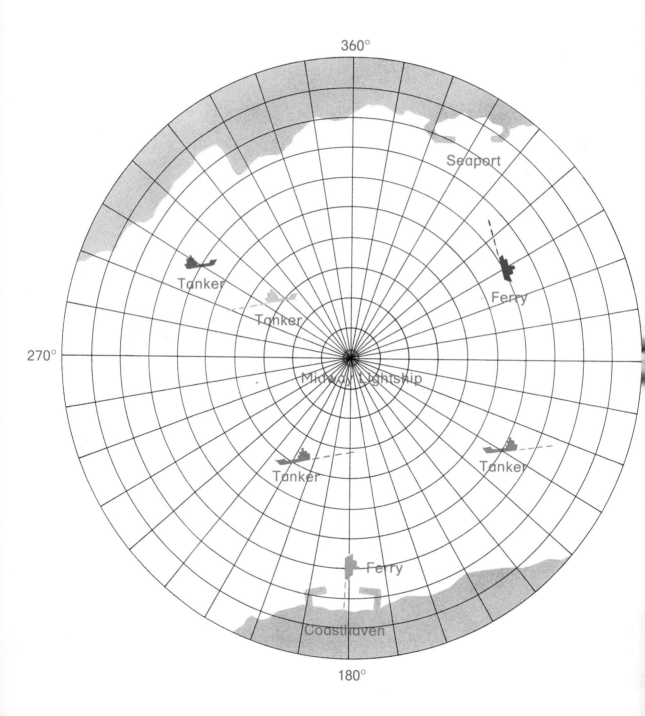

Bearing up

Bearings are angles measured in a clockwise direction starting from North.

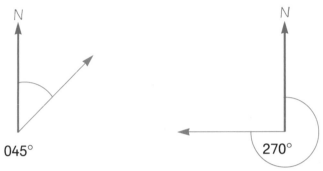

045°   270°

If the angle is less than 100°, we put a 0 at the beginning, so all bearings have 3 digits.

The bearing of the purple ferry from the lightship is 060°, the pink ferry is 180°.

What are the bearings of these from the lightship?

1. The yellow tanker

2. The orange tanker

3. The green tanker

4. The red tanker

5. Coasthaven

6. If the pink ferry travels 1 mile on a bearing of 180°, where will it get to?

7. If the green tanker travels 13 miles on a bearing of 030°, where will it get to?

8. What is the bearing of the purple ferry from the red tanker?

There is more about bearings on page 72.

Measuring angles accurately

There are 10 divisions between
the 10° markers on a protractor.
They are used to measure angles
more accurately.
Each fifth division is made
slightly longer to help you read
the measurement.

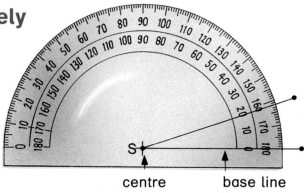

centre   base line

Estimate, to the nearest 10°, the size of these angles.
Then measure them accurately.
Write your estimate and measure in a chart.

We can write
the angle
joining line RS
to line ST as RST.
RST is 18°.

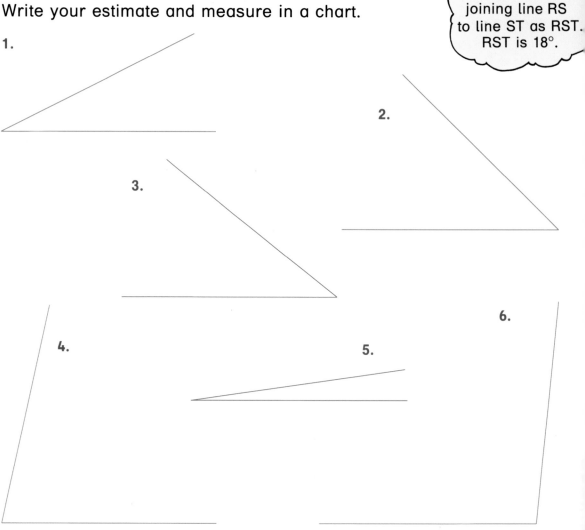

1.

2.

3.

4.

5.

6.

Angles in polygons

Measure all the angles in these polygons. Then, for each
polygon add up the angles. Count the number of sides.

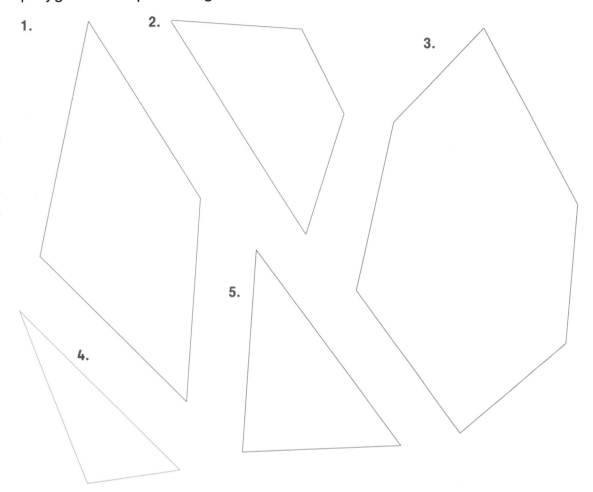

1.

2.

3.

5.

4.

6. What do you notice about the sum of the angles in:
the triangles?
the quadrilaterals?
the hexagon?

7. Test your answers to question **6.** by drawing your own shapes
and measuring the angles.

There is more about angles on page 74.

An activities weekend

On an activities weekend children could choose any 6 from these 10 possibilities:

1. abseiling

2. canoeing

3. wind-surfing

4. pony-trekking

5. parascending

6. archery

7. orienteering

8. climbing

9. dinghy sailing

10. water-skiing

The children's choices are shown on page 37.

Children's options

These are the options the children chose:

Simon:	2	4	1	8	10	6
Sarah:	10	1	5	3	9	7
Kim:	7	4	3	10	9	2
Umeed:	10	4	6	2	7	5
Rachel:	4	8	9	3	2	10
Timmy:	9	6	7	10	4	3
Nina:	5	4	6	9	2	1
Kerry:	1	4	2	7	5	9
Kirk:	4	6	2	3	8	10
Lee:	10	7	6	3	4	9

1. Design a chart to show more clearly the children and the activities each has chosen.

2. Use your chart to list how many children will be doing each activity.

3. Which 2 children have chosen to do exactly the same activities?

4. Carry out a survey in your class to find out which 6 activities children would like to do. Compare this with Simon and Sarah's class. Are the popular activities the same?

How many words per day?

4 children wanted to find out how many words
they wrote in a day at school.

On Friday they had 5 lessons: pottery, science,
design technology, religious studies and geography.
After each lesson they wrote down the number of
words they had written. Here are their results:

Emma: 0, 66, 10, 105, 82

Claire: 0, 81, 23, 75, 86

Sean: 0, 52, 8, 99, 128

Tony: 0, 34, 11, 53, 62

1. Make a chart to show clearly the names of the children
    and the number of words they wrote in each lesson.

Use your chart to discover:

2. who wrote most altogether.

3. which lesson required most writing.

4. Collect similar information from friends in your class.
    Organise the information into a chart showing who
    writes most and in which lesson people generally
    write most.

How good is your memory?

You can use this picture to test people's memories.
Ask them to look at it for 10 seconds. Then cover it up.
Ask them to write down as many objects as they can
remember.

1. Do this activity with several different friends.
   Design a chart to show their results clearly.

Use your chart to discover:

2. if any objects are remembered more easily than
   others.

3. if any objects are not remembered at all.

4. Repeat the experiment at different times of day.
   Do people remember more in the morning
   or the afternoon?

Let's find out – food

These 2 pages should give you some ideas
about things you can investigate to do with food.

Choose one you are really interested in.
You will need to decide:

what data to collect

how to collect it

how to organise it and show your results clearly

how to interpret the data.

1. **Smarties investigation**

   What colour do you get
   most of in a tube of
   Smarties?
   Is the result the same for
   lots of tubes of Smarties?
   (If you prefer, you may
   use other coloured sweets
   such as jelly babies.)

2. **Chocolate investigation**

   Weight for weight,
   what is the cheapest
   chocolate bar?
   Instead of chocolate
   bars, you could look at
   crisps or yoghurts or
   cartons of drink.

Handling data contexts   Unit 1   Collecting, processing, representing and interpreting data in the context of food

3. From potato to snack

Compare the price of a potato with packets of crisps.
How many crisps can you get from a potato?
What does the average crisp weigh?
Are the results the same for other potato snacks
like hoops and chipsticks?

4. Eating habits

How much of your day do
you spend eating?

Do you spend more time
or less time than your
friends?

In your school, are
younger children slower
eaters than older
children?

The probability scale

Remember: the probability scale can be shown as a number line from 0 to 1.

0 is impossible, 1 is certain, 0.5 is an even chance.

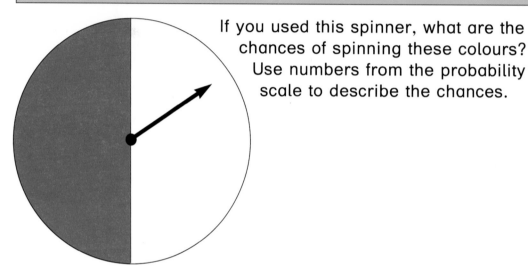

If you used this spinner, what are the chances of spinning these colours? Use numbers from the probability scale to describe the chances.

1. red

2. yellow

3. either red or white

4. white

If you toss a coin, what are the probabilities of these happening?

5. heads

6. it will hover in mid-air

7. tails

8. it will land eventually

9. it will change its value in mid-air

Probability and fractions

Remember: you can also use fractions to describe probability.

On this spinner, there are six colours. This means there are six possible outcomes. Each outcome is equally likely, so to spin an orange, there is 1 chance out of 6. This can be written as $\frac{1}{6}$.

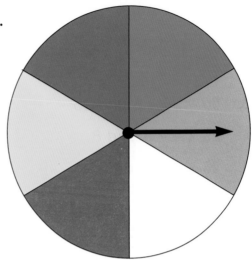

Write the fractions which describe the probability of spinning these colours on these spinners:

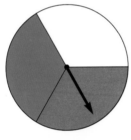

1. red   2. blue   3. white

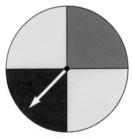

4. blue   5. yellow   6. black

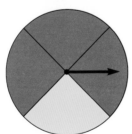

7. yellow   8. red   9. blue

There is more about probability on page 82.

Are they the same?

Here are some pairs of expressions.

Write whether each pair gives the same or a different result.

1. $2 + 3 \times 4$ and $3 \times 4 + 2$

2. $2 \times 12 \div 3$ and $12 \div 3 \times 2$

3. $50 - 25 - 5$ and $25 - 5 - 50$

4. $25 \times 4 - 8$ and $8 - 25 \times 4$

5. $25 \times 4 \div 5$ and $5 \div 25 \times 4$

Copy these. Fill in the operations and brackets to make true statements.

6. $7 \quad 3 \quad 5 \quad 4 = 46$

7. $7 \quad 3 \quad 5 \quad 4 = 22$

8. $7 \quad 3 \quad 5 \quad 4 = 24$

9. $7 \quad 3 \quad 5 \quad 4 = 80$

10. $7 \quad 3 \quad 5 \quad 4 = 200$

11. Choose 4 digits of your own.

Use brackets and operations as in questions 6. to 10.

Make as many different numbers as you can.
Choose one of the numbers you have made.

Can you make it in more than one way using the same 4 digits?

3-digit target numbers

Use any of the cards in each box to make the target numbers.
You can only use a card once.
You may use brackets and any of the operations.

1.

9	25	8	5	6	3

322

2.

75	2	7	4	1	8

833

3.

50	9	6	2	3	5

485

4.

100	6	5	3	4	1

663

5.

25	10	7	6	5	2

199

6.

50	8	7	4	1	3

533

Make some cards of your own.

Use them to play a game with a friend.

One player chooses 6 cards.
The other player chooses a
3-digit target number.
The first person to make the
target number wins.

Big number products

The numbers in the grid are products of pairs of red numbers. For example,

$98\,412 = 354 \times 278$.

One number in the grid is the square of one of the red numbers.
Estimate first, then use your calculator to check which red numbers multiply to make each number in the grid. Write them down.

429

995

536

354

278

678

98 412	119 262	229 944	426 855
189 744	276 610	990 025	363 408
149 008	533 320	188 484	674 610
151 866	290 862	352 230	240 012

This can be played as a game if you make your own grid.

Players take turns to estimate which 2 numbers multiply to make a number in the grid.
Check with a calculator.
If the estimate is correct, the number is covered with a counter.

The first player to cover 3 numbers in a column, row or diagonal wins.

Population explosion

When comparing populations you need to think in millions! For example, 26 000 000 > 21 500 000.

Chart of European population figures			
Belgium	9 500 000	Holland	14 500 000
Denmark	5 120 000	Italy	57 300 000
France	55 500 000	Spain	38 800 000
Germany	77 600 000	United Kingdom	56 100 000

Use the chart to compare these countries' populations.
Use < or >.

1. Italy and France
2. Germany and Spain
3. UK and Belgium
4. Holland and Denmark
5. UK and Germany
6. Denmark and Belgium
7. Which country has the smallest population?
8. Which country has the largest population?

Prime factors

Remember: a prime number is a number that can only be divided by itself and 1.

Prime factors are factors which are also prime numbers.

The factors of 15 are 1, 3, 5 and 15.

1 is not usually counted as a prime number.

3 and 5 are both prime numbers, therefore the prime factors of 15 are 3 and 5.

The factors of 12 are 1, 2, 3, 4, 6, 12.

2 and 3 are the prime factors of 12.

1. The factors of 8 are 1, 2, 4 and 8.
    Which of these is a prime factor?

Find the prime factors of these numbers:

2. 10   3. 24   4. 21

5. 72   6. 35   7. 81

8. 18   9. 52   10. 16

Numbers as prime factors

Numbers can be expressed in a special way, using their prime factors.

The factors of 10 are 1, 2, 5, 10.

The prime factors of 10 are 2 and 5.

We can express 10 as the product of its prime factors, $10 = 2 \times 5$.

The factors of 12 are 1, 2, 3, 4, 6 and 12.

Its prime factors are 2 and 3.

12 can be expressed as the product of its prime factors, but one of them has to be used more than once.

$$12 = 2 \times 2 \times 3$$

Find the prime factors of these numbers.
Show how to use the prime factors to express the numbers.

1. 14   2. 27   3. 42

4. 50   5. 38   6. 33

7. 28   8. 45   9. 56

There is more about factors on page 88.

Comparing positive and negative numbers

If you start at 3 on this number line, and count back 5, you land on −2.

−4 −3 −2 −1 0 1 2 3 4

Use this number line to work out which number you land on when you follow the directions below.

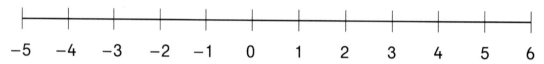

−5 −4 −3 −2 −1 0 1 2 3 4 5 6

1. Start on 3, count back 6

2. Start on −4, count on 3

3. Start on −2, count on 7

4. Start on 5, count back 5

5. Start on −1, count on 2

6. Start on 2, count back 4

7. Start on 4, count back 2

8. Start on −5, count on 4

If you count along a number line from left to right, the numbers get bigger.

If you count back from right to left, the numbers get smaller.

For example, −3 < 1, (negative three is less than one).

Use < or > to make these true statements:

9. −4 ☐ −2

10. 3 ☐ −1

11. −1 ☐ −3

12. 2 ☐ 5

13. −4 ☐ 2

14. −2 ☐ 0

Time lines

This is a time line of Anthony's life so far.
It also shows things that happened before
he was born.

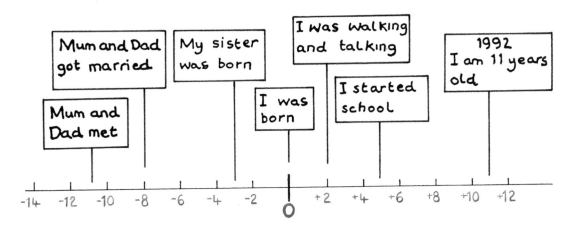

What happened at these points on the time line?

1. −11   **2.** +5   **3.** −3   **4.** +2

5. Where on the time line did Anthony's mum and
dad get married?

6. Which year was that?

7. In which year was his sister born?

8. Make your own time line. Use 0 (zero) for when you
were born.
On the + side mark the main events of your life so far.
On the − side mark your family's main events before
you were born.

Try, then improve

You will need a calculator.

Sunil used his calculator and his knowledge to solve this problem.

Which number, when multiplied by 24, gives the answer 102?

Unfortunately the division key on his calculator was missing!

He knew that 4 x 25 = 100.

So he used his calculator to try:

  too big. So he improved by trying...

  too small. So he improved by trying...

  too big. So he improved by trying...

   just too small. He tried...

    just too big.

1. Continue Sunil's problem by trying a number between 4.2 and 4.3. Use the same method to find the numbers covered by the clouds.

2. ( ) x 22 = 55   3. ( ) x 28 = 91   4. ( ) x 64 = 304

5. ( ) x 34 = 221   6. ( ) x 56 = 315

Make up some more cloud problems for a friend.

Fractions to decimals and back again

Remember: if you use a calculator, you can change a fraction like $\frac{1}{4}$ to a decimal by dividing 1 by 4.

$1 \div 4 = 0.25$

If you now multiply 0.25 by 4 it will return to 1.

We say 0.25 is the reciprocal of 4.

To find the reciprocal of any number, divide 1 by it.

1. Make a chart of all the reciprocals of the numbers from 1 to 10. Write them to 2 and 3 decimal places. (Use a calculator.)

Number	Reciprocals	
	2 decimal places	3 decimal places
1	$(1 \div 1)$ 1.00	1.000
2	$(1 \div 2)$ 0.50	0.500
3	$(1 \div 3)$ 0.33	0.333

2. Multiply the reciprocals by the original number. Why do some seem not to return exactly to 1?

There is more about decimals on page 90.

Find the fraction

Remember: to find $\frac{3}{5}$ of 20, first find $\frac{1}{5}$ by dividing by 5.

$\frac{1}{5}$ of 20 is 4, so $\frac{3}{5}$ is 12.

The whole set of 20

$\frac{3}{5}$ of the set is 12

Write these amounts:

1. $\frac{2}{5}$ of £2.50

2. $\frac{1}{4}$ of a metre

3. $\frac{3}{10}$ of 2 litres

4. $\frac{3}{8}$ of 32 kilograms

5. $\frac{3}{4}$ of £4.80

6. $\frac{7}{8}$ of a kilometre

7. $\frac{6}{20}$ of 60p

8. $\frac{2}{3}$ of £39

9. $\frac{5}{6}$ of 480 g

10. $\frac{5}{8}$ of 100 m

Everyday fractions

Remember: sometimes you can find a simpler way to write a fraction. For example $\frac{4}{20} = \frac{2}{10} = \frac{1}{5}$.

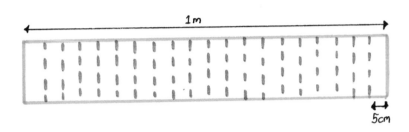

Fold a metre strip into 5 cm lengths.

1. Make a chart like this to show all the fractions of a metre.

length	fraction	equivalent fractions
5 cm	$\frac{1}{20}$	—
10 cm	$\frac{2}{20}$	$\frac{1}{10}$
15 cm	$\frac{3}{20}$	—
20 cm	$\frac{4}{20}$	$\frac{2}{10}$ $\frac{1}{5}$

2. Work out how long you spend each day eating, sleeping, working, playing, watching television, and so on. Write each one as a fraction of the day.

There is more about fractions on page 94.

Fractions and ratios

Remember: 3:1 means 'for every 3 of one kind there is
        1 of another kind'.

This box contains plain chocolates, milk chocolates
and white chocolates.

Write these as fractions of the whole box.

1. plain chocolates   2. milk chocolates   3. white chocolates

What are the ratios of:

4. plain chocolates to milk chocolates

5. white chocolates to milk chocolates

6. plain chocolates to white chocolates

There are 23 jelly babies in a bag.

There are 3 colours, yellow, red and black.

There are 3 times as many yellows as blacks.

There are 5 times as many yellows as reds.

How many jelly babies are:

7. yellow?   8. red?   9. black?

School ratios

32 children use this classroom.

14 are boys and

18 are girls.

They have 8 tables and 32 chairs.

In the painting area there are
12 pallettes and 40 brushes.

The class library has 120 books.

The resource area has 50 felt-tipped pens,
48 crayons and 10 rubbers.

Write these ratios.

1. children to tables
2. children to chairs
3. books to children
4. brushes to children
5. crayons to children
6. children to pallettes
7. felt-tipped pens to children
8. children to rubbers

Make a survey of your own classroom and write ratios
for how many children there are to each kind of resource.

There is more about ratio on page 98.

Growing triangles

You will need triangular paper.

Here is a single equilateral triangle, drawn on triangular paper.

To make the next size up, you need to add 3 more triangles.

1. How many triangles do you need to make the next size of equilateral triangle?

2. Continue to grow the triangles. Keep a chart like this:

Triangle size	Number of triangles added	Total number of triangles used
1 x 1 x 1	1	1
2 x 2 x 2	3	4

3. Describe the patterns of numbers in each column of the chart.

Cube patterns

Here is a solid shape.
It is made from 5 cubes.

To make it grow, one cube is
added to each stem.
There are now 9 cubes.

1. Continue the pattern. Make it grow by adding cubes.
   Keep a chart like this:

Shape number	Number of cubes added	Total number of cubes used
1		5
2	4	9
3		

2. Describe the pattern of numbers in each column.

3. How many cubes would there be in the 100th shape.

4. Devise your own cube pattern.
   Keep a chart of how it grows.
   Describe the number patterns in each column.

Making an area of squares graph

> Remember: to find the area of a square you multiply its length by its breadth. As the length and breadth are the same you can use the formula:
> Area = Length x Length or $a = l^2$.

1. Copy and continue this chart up to at least 10 cm.

2. Copy this graph. Use your chart to continue the graph. Show the length on the x axis and the corresponding area on the y axis.

length of side	area $a = l^2$
1 cm	1 cm^2
2 cm	4 cm^2
3 cm	9 cm^2
4 cm	16 cm^2

3. Describe the shape of your graph.

4. Use the graph to find the approximate area of a square 5.5 cm x 5.5 cm.

5. Use the graph to find the length of the side of a square with an area of 20.25 cm^2.

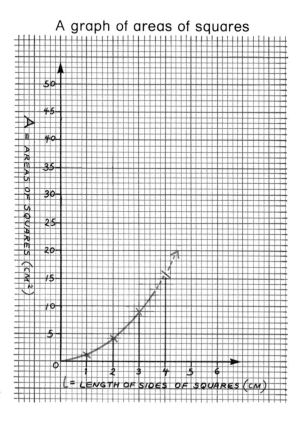

A graph of areas of squares

Making a circumference graph

> Remember: to find the circumference of a circle you can use the
> formula: $\pi \times d = c$
>
> $\pi = 3.14$ correct to 2 decimal places

1. Copy and continue the chart and the graph below to at least a diameter of 10 cm.

diameter d	circumference c
1 cm	3.14 cm
2 cm	6.28 cm
3 cm	9.42 cm

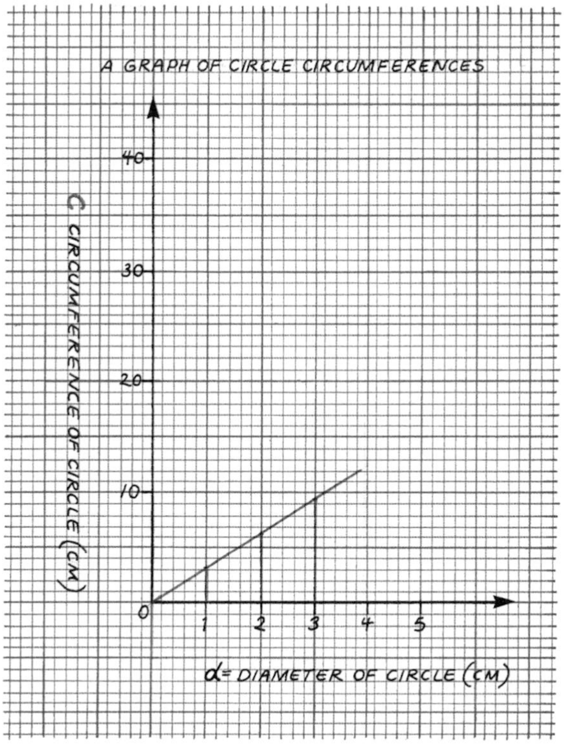

A GRAPH OF CIRCLE CIRCUMFERENCES

C CIRCUMFERENCE OF CIRCLE (CM)

d = DIAMETER OF CIRCLE (CM)

2. Mark the point on your graph which shows the circumference if the diameter is 4.5 cm.

3. Use your graph to find the approximate diameter of a circle with a circumference of 20.5 cm.

4. Describe your graph.

Old money, new money

Before 1971 Britain's currency was pounds (£), shillings (s) and pence (d). The graph below shows the conversion between old pence (d) and new pence (p). For example, x shows that 50p was worth 120d.

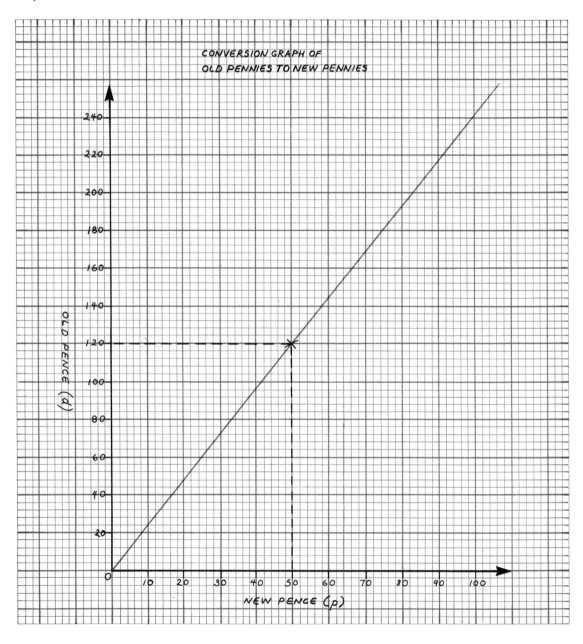

Conversions

There used to be 12 old pennies in a shilling.
Use the graph on page 62 to convert these
amounts into new money.

1. 2 shillings
2. 20 shillings
3. 5 shillings
4. 15 shillings
5. 12 shillings
6. 9 shillings

What were these coins worth in old money?

7. 20p
8. 10p
9. 2p
10. 1p

Make your own conversion graph.

In Britain there are 100p in £1.

In the USA there are 100 cents(c) in 1 dollar $.

Draw a conversion graph between dollars and pounds
if £1 is worth $1.50.

Use it to find out how many pounds you would get for:

11. $82.50
12. $121.50
13. $68.25
14. $146.25

Find out what the current exchange rate is between £ and $.
How would you need to change your graph?

9-pin triangles

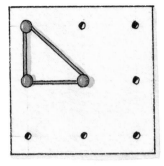

This triangle has an area of $\frac{1}{2}$ a unit.

What are the areas of these triangles?

1.
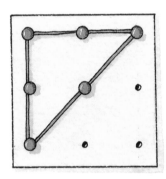

2.
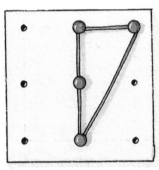

3.
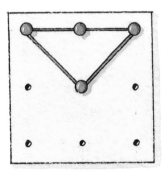

4.
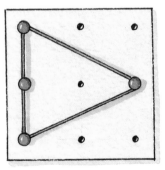

Make some more triangles on a 9-pin geoboard.
Work out their areas.

Pairs of triangles

Two congruent (identical) triangles can make
a parallelogram.

Copy each triangle twice. Put the 2 pieces together
to make a parallelogram.

Find the area of the parallelogram and the triangle.

Remember: the area of a parallelogram is base x height.

1.

2.

3.

4. Draw 4 different triangles each with an area of 6 cm^2.

There is more about area on page 102.

Cutting and folding

1. Fold a piece of paper in four as shown. Cut off the corner. Unfold the paper. How many lines of symmetry has the hole in the paper?

   What is the shape of the hole?

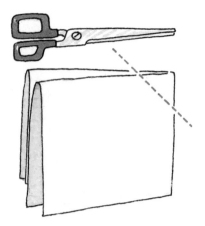

2. Now fold a sheet like this and cut off the corner. Describe the shape of the hole.

   How many lines of symmetry has the hole got?

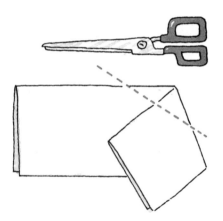

3. Fold and cut paper to make different shaped holes. Try to predict how many lines of symmetry the hole will have.
   Draw them on to the piece you have cut out of the paper.

Polyominoes

A triomino is a shape made up from 3 squares. There are only 2 different ones.

The rectangle has 2 lines of symmetry.

The L-shape (hexagon) has only 1 line of symmetry.

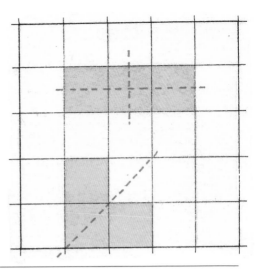

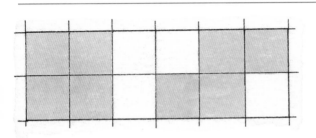

Here are 2 tetrominoes.

A tetromino is made up from 4 squares.

1. Copy these on to squared paper. Then find all the other tetrominoes you can.

2. Name the shape of each tetromino. For example, square, hexagon, and so on.

3. Draw the lines of symmetry for each tetromino.

Here are 2 pentominoes.

A pentomino is made from 5 squares.

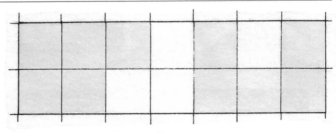

4. Copy these on to squared paper and find all the other pentominoes you can.

5. Draw the lines of symmetry for each pentomino.

National flags

This flag of St. Patrick has 2 lines of symmetry.

If it were lifted and rotated it would fit into its own outline in 2 positions.
So it has rotational symmetry of order 2.

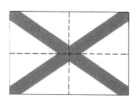

For these flags, write the country, number of lines of symmetry and order of rotational symmetry.

> Remember: order 1 means no rotational symmetry.

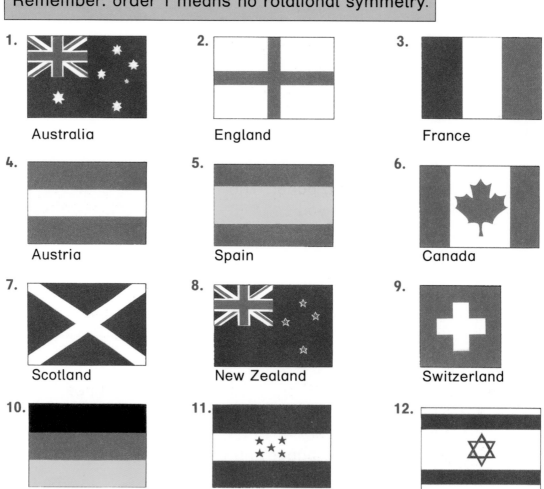

1. Australia

2. England

3. France

4. Austria

5. Spain

6. Canada

7. Scotland

8. New Zealand

9. Switzerland

10. Germany

11. Honduras

12. Israel

Symmetry in digital roots

X	1	2	3	4	5	6	7	8
1	1	2	3	4	5	6	7	8
2	2	4	6	8	1			
3	3	6	9	3			3	
4	4	8	3	7				
5	5	1						
6	6			6				
7	7						4	
8	8							

This is a partly completed tables square.

The answers have been converted to digital roots.

Remember: to find a digital root, you add the digits of the answer.

8 x 6 = 48   4 + 8 = 12   1 + 2 = 3

3 is the digital root of 48.

1. Copy and complete the table. Describe any symmetrical pattern of numbers you see, for example about the diagonals of the square.

2. Join the centres of all the '1' squares, using straight lines. What is the name of the overall shape? How many lines of symmetry has this shape?

3. Repeat question 2. using other numbers. Describe your results.

Co-ordinates and quadrants

The x and y axes divide the graph paper into 4 parts.
These are called quadrants.

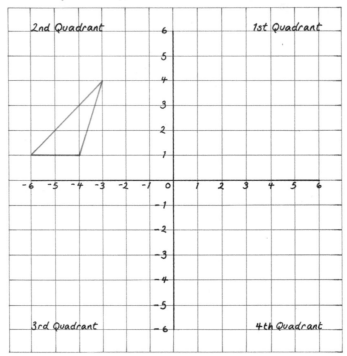

The red triangle is in the second quadrant.

The x co-ordinate of one of its vertices is −6.

The y co-ordinate of that vertex is 1.

So the co-ordinates of the vertex are (−6, 1).

1.   Write the co-ordinates of the other two vertices.

     Now answer these questions about the red triangle:

2.   Are the x co-ordinates positive or negative?

3.   Are the y co-ordinates positive or negative?

4.   What can you say about the x and y co-ordinates of
     any point in the second quadrant?

Moving triangles

Copy the axes and triangle on page 70 on to graph paper.

1. If we add 8 to each x co-ordinate of the red triangle, but keep the y co-ordinate the same, we get (2, 1) (4, 1) (5, 4).

   Draw a new triangle with these new co-ordinates.

2. Which quadrant is it in?

3. What can you say about the x and y co-ordinates of any point in this quadrant?

4. Now subtract 7 from each y co-ordinate of your new triangle and draw another triangle.

5. What can you say about the x and y co-ordinate of any point in the fourth quadrant?

6. Draw a triangle in the third quadrant and write the co-ordinates of its vertices.

7. What can you say about the co-ordinates of any point in the third quadrant?

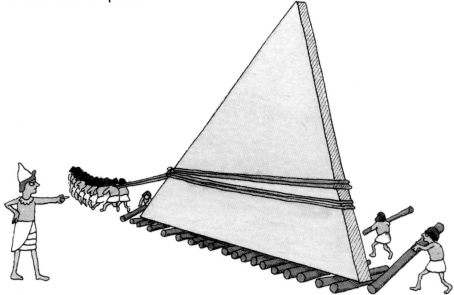

A flying tour of Scotland

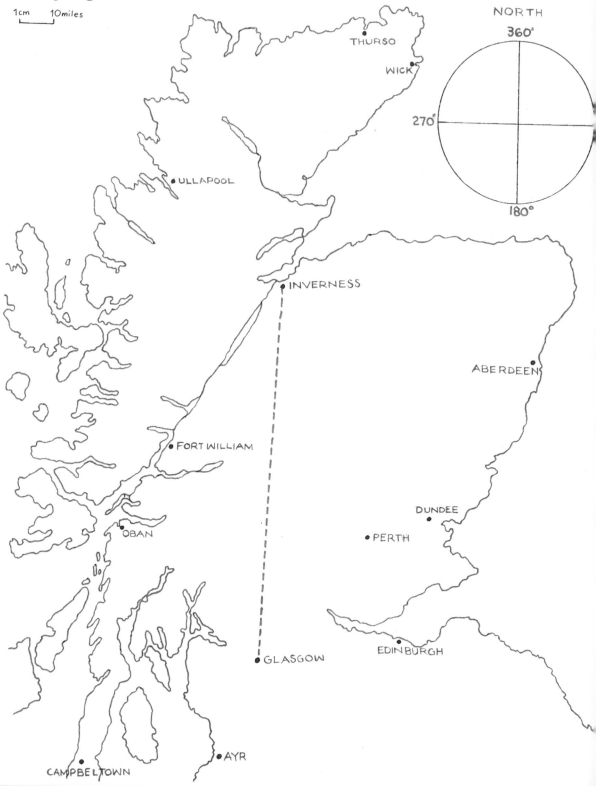

Location and transformation of shapes   Unit 2   Map of part of Scotland

Pre-flight planning

You will need a ruler and protractor.

Remember: a bearing is an angle measured clockwise from North. For example, the bearing of Glasgow from Inverness is 190°.

Bearings have three figures, so we write 45° as a bearing of 045°.

Write these bearings to the nearest 10°.

1. Glasgow to Edinburgh

2. Perth to Wick

3. Fort William to Glasgow

4. Campbeltown to Aberdeen

5. Thurso to Oban

6. Ullapool to Dundee

Write all the bearings you would need to use for these flying tours:

7. Glasgow to Dundee to Aberdeen to Inverness to Thurso.

8. Edinburgh to Ayr to Campbeltown to Oban to Ullapool to Wick.

9. Make up your own flying tour of Scotland and write all the bearings you will need to use.

Drawing angles

You will need a protractor and a ruler.

Measure these angles and lines carefully.
Then draw them.

1.

2.

3.

4.

5.

6.

Draw these angles:

7. 7°   8. 48°   9. 35°   10. 88°

Wheels

This wheel has 3 red spokes. They are equally spaced. If you join the ends of the spokes, they form a large equilateral triangle.

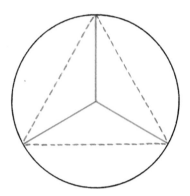

1. Measure the angles at the centre of the wheel. What do you notice?

2. Measure the angles of the large blue triangle. What do you notice?

3. Draw your own wheel with 4 equally spaced spokes. Measure the angles at the centre. Join the ends of the spokes. What shape do you make?

4. Do the same for wheels with 5 spokes, 6 spokes, 8 spokes and 10 spokes. Describe the angles and shapes you make.

Class information

Name	Date of birth	Height in centimetres	Weight in kilograms
Veronique	15/09/81	157	42.5
Bernard	22/10/81	159.5	50
Melissa	6/11/81	156.5	47.5
John	11/11/81	157	49.5
Shaheen	19/12/81	150	35
Kiran	22/12/81	159.5	51.5
Gurpreet	15/01/82	158	46
William	31/01/82	155.5	49.5
Daniel	02/05/82	162.5	54.5
Martin	09/05/82	147	41.5
Louise	05/06/82	156	48
Anna	28/07/82	154	45.5
Amandeep	12/08/82	159.5	53
Sanjiv	19/08/82	157.5	45
Simon	26/08/82	157.5	47
Kathleen	15/09/82	163	52.5
Yasmin	04/11/82	154.5	44
Kai Chun	05/12/82	146	37.5
Ashley	18/12/82	162.5	50
Lee	28/01/83	159	46
Janica	25/02/83	158.5	43.5
Nicola	10/03/83	157	48.5

Use this database for the work on page 77.

Showing the information

> Remember: a frequency table can be used to group and order data.

The data on page 76 was collected at the beginning of January 1993.

The children's ages have been partly organised into a frequency table.

Age Range	Number of children
9 yrs 9m ≤ age < 10 yrs 0m	3
10 yrs 0m ≤ age < 10 yrs 3m	3
10 yrs 3m ≤ age < 10 yrs 6m	5
10 yrs 6m ≤ age < 10 yrs 9m	
10 yrs 9m ≤ age < 11 yrs 0m	
11 yrs 0m ≤ age < 11 yrs 3m	
11 yrs 3m ≤ age < 11 yrs 6m	1

Notice that the data has been grouped into equal age ranges (class intervals), of three months.

Notice also how carefully the age ranges have been labelled. This is to make it absolutely clear into which range each child's age falls.

1. Complete the frequency table for the children's ages.

2. Create a frequency table for children's heights. Decide what height ranges to group data into, and label the ranges carefully.

3. Now create a frequency table for children's weights.

> There is more about frequency tables on the next page.

Sunflower survey

Children in a small village school each grew a sunflower to see how tall the flowers would grow. They planted seeds in April and measured their sunflowers in September.
Here are the heights (in centimetres):

98, 102, 155, 220, 253, 94, 149, 190, 192, 234, 251, 112, 165, 249, 252, 132, 171, 230, 250, 127, 186, 201, 105, 175, 111, 173, 207, 150, 185, 200, 206, 119, 162, 198, 204, 142, 176, 154, 205, 189, 173, 144, 200, 164, 190, 100, 178, 151, 112, 156

They made a frequency table like this:

50 cm ≤ h < 100 cm	100 cm ≤ h < 150 cm	150 cm ≤
II	LHI LHI III	LHI
2	13	

1. Complete the table.

2. Use the information in the table to make a frequency diagram.

3. How tall are the sunflowers in the modal class (the class containing most sunflowers)?

4. Calculate the mean height of the sunflowers.

5. Is the mean height in the modal class?

Potatoes

Children weighed each potato in a bag of potatoes.

Here is their data collection sheet:

375g, 225g, 110g, 75g, 100g, 80g, 50g, 225g, 280g, 125g, 125g, 175g, 430g, 275g, 200g, 225g, 210g, 110g, 100g, 180g, 250g, 110g, 220g, 100g, 175g, 180g, 200g, 190g, 75g, 100g

1. Find the mean weight of the potatoes.

2. Order the weights from smallest to largest and find the median weight.

3. What is the mode weight?

4. Organise the data into a frequency table. (You will need to use equal class intervals.)

5. Which class interval has the highest frequency (the modal class)?

6. Now draw a frequency diagram to display the data clearly.

7. Describe the shape of your diagram. Is it symmetrical, skewed or of no particular shape?

You may like to make your own survey of other vegetables or fruit.

How to predict probabilities

We can predict probability in different ways:

Theoretically – if outcomes seem equally likely, we can often work out probabilities fairly accurately.

For example, it looks as though the chance of spinning a blue on this spinner is $\frac{1}{3}$.

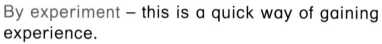

From experience – we can take note of what has happened before and use the information to predict what will happen. For example, if a big black cloud is overhead the chances of getting wet are more than evens.

By experiment – this is a quick way of gaining experience.
We try something many times to see what usually happens.
For example, if we throw a drawing pin in the air 100 times and it lands on its back 25 times, we can say the probability of it landing on its back is about $\frac{1}{4}$.

How would you predict the probabilities of these things happening: theoretically, from experience or by experiment?

1. If I tease the cat, it will scratch me.

2. If I toss 2 coins, they will land one head and one tail.

3. If I roll a dice, I will get a 6.

4. If I spin a bottle, it will end up pointing away from me.

5. If I pick a playing card from a pack, it will be an ace.

6. If it is a frosty morning, the bird bath will be frozen.

Some probability experiments

Try one or more of these probability experiments.
Predict what might happen before you start them.

1. Make a series of predictions like:

    'The next person to come into the class will be a man.'
    or
    'The next car to pass the school will have a passenger.'

    Keep a record of your predictions and whether
    they came true or not. Do you get better the
    more predictions you make?

2. Set up a bag like this. (You could use
    cubes instead of balls.) What are the
    chances of pulling out a green ball?
    Pull out a ball several times and keep
    a list of your results.

    Was your prediction correct?

3. 'When a paper cup is thrown up into
    the air it will land on its base.'

    Predict the probability of this
    happening. Then find somewhere
    suitable to test your prediction.
    What do you discover?

4. Open any book at any page. Close your eyes and,
    with your finger, touch a word.

    Test this statement:
    'The word I touch will have 4 letters.'

    Can you predict beforehand how many letters
    the word will have?

    What is the most common length of word in your book?

 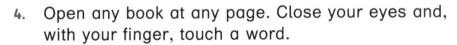 There is more about probability on page 124.

Let's find out – the library

These 2 pages should give you some ideas about things you can investigate to do with your class, school or local library.

Choose one you are really interested in. You will need to decide:

what question you want to answer.

what data you need to answer it.

how to collect the data.

how to interpret the data.

how to present it to convince others.

---

1. **Your favourite books**

Does the library have enough of the kind of books you like?

You might be interested in aircraft or motorbikes, dancing or ice-skating.

You may have a favourite author.

Find out how many of a particular book there are and how they are organised.

If you do need more books, how can you obtain them?

2. Tatty books

Some books in your library may be falling apart. Is it the most popular books that get damaged quickly?

How many books in your library are falling apart?

How many can be repaired and how many need replacing?

3. Library organisation

This library looks crowded, noisy and disorganised.

What is your library like?

Are the books easy to find?

Do people put them back in the right place?

Is there enough furniture to sit and read quietly?

Do too many people go there at the same time?

(Try to find some solutions for these problems, as well.)

Many methods of multiplication

Over thousands of years, different cultures have devised their own methods of multiplying large numbers.

The Egyptians used doubling.

To multiply 326 x 21 they would make a list which doubled.

$$326 \times 1 = 326$$

doubled 326 x 2 = 652

doubled 326 x 4 = 1304

doubled 326 x 8 = 2608

doubled 326 x 16 = 5216

To find the answer, they would add the products of the numbers which added to 21. In this case,
16 + 4 + 1 = 21,
so the answer is 5216 + 1304 + 326 = 6846.

Use the Egyptian method to solve these problems:

1. 547 x 23
2. 258 x 37

3. 876 x 26
4. 425 x 32

5. Use the Egyptian method to solve this problem:

The James family spends £136 per week on groceries. How much do they spend in a year?

Solve these your own way

Solve these multiplications.

Look carefully at the numbers and decide whether to do them in your head or work them out on paper. You may be able to work out a quick method.

1. 136 x 21
2. 63 x 101
3. 51 x 226
4. 81 x 381
5. 109 x 55
6. 499 x 101

7. Mrs Harris' mortgage is £476 per month. How much does she have to pay per year.

8. The fishing club flew to Ireland for a competition. The fare was £119 each. 24 people went. How much was the total cost?

9. Carpet tiles come in packs of 12. Mr. Patel used 211 packs to carpet a shop. How many tiles did he lay?

10. If each carpet tile cost 34p, how much did Mr. Patel's tiles cost altogether?

For at least one of the multiplications explain to a friend exactly how you did it. Write your explanation down.

Writing numbers the Roman way

The digits we use are:

0 1 2 3 4 5 6 7 8 9

These are Hindu-Arabic numerals and with them we represent all our numbers.

127   10 809   32 564 803

The Romans used capital letters as numerals:

I	V	X	L	C	D	M
1	5	10	50	100	500	1000

They put them together to make their numbers:

I = 1 II = 2 III = 3 IV = 4 V = 5
VI = 6 VII = 7 VIII = 8 IX = 9

Putting a letter after a bigger one means you add it.

XI = 11 LXX = 70 CLXI = 161

Putting a letter before a bigger one means you subtract it.

IL = 49 XC = 90

So CCXVI = 216, MCMXIV = 1914

What numbers do these Roman numerals represent?

1. LXVIII   2. DCXXII   3. XL

4. MDCCXIV   5. MMI   6. MCMXCIII

Write these numbers in Roman numerals:

7. 2025   8. 89   9. 3408

Egyptian numerals

The ancient Egyptians wrote the numbers up to 9 using strokes:

1	2	3	4	5	6	7	8	9

When they reached 10 they used /\

For 100 they used ⟨9⟩   For 1000 ⚶

53 was written ∧∧∧
                ∧∧ |||

What do these Egyptian numerals show?

1. ∧∧∧∧|||
      ∧∧∧||

2. 999 |||
       99 ∧∧|||

3. ⚶ 9999∧∧∧|||||
       999 ∧∧∧|||

4. ⚶⚶ 9|||
        |||
        |||

Write these using Egyptian numerals:

5. 999   **6.** 13   **7.** 3333   **8.** 4001

Factorise it!

Remember: to express a number in terms of its factors is to factorise it.

If we prime factorise a number, we express it in terms of its prime factors only.

For example, if we factorise 8 we write 2 x 4.

If we prime factorise 8 we write 2 x 2 x 2.

One way of showing this is by using factor trees.

For example, start with any pair of factors of 36 and factorise them. Carry on until you get prime factors.

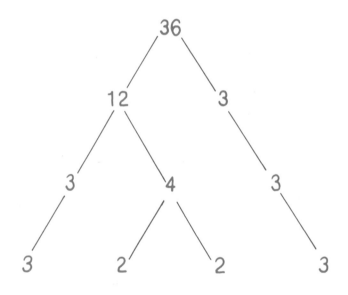

$$36 = 2 \times 2 \times 3 \times 3$$

Make factor trees starting with other pairs of factors for 36.

More factor trees

Copy and complete these factor trees.

1.

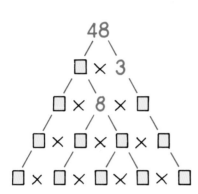

2.

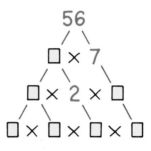

3.

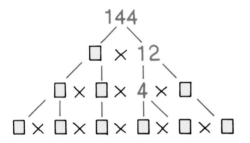

4.

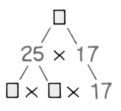

5.

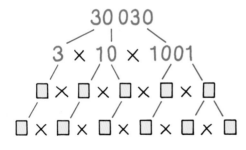

6.

4199
13 × ☐
☐ × ☐ × ☐

Make factor trees to find the prime factors of these numbers.

7. 72   **8.** 42   **9.** 39   **10.** 63

Showing decimals on a number line

To show a decimal like 3.637 on a number line:

First make a number line between 3 and 4 showing tenths.

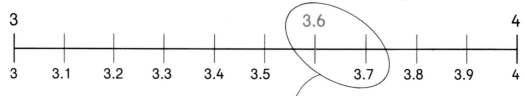

Then look at the section between 3.6 and 3.7 in hundredths.

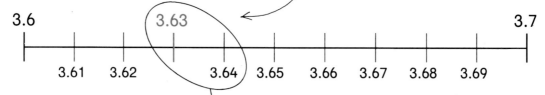

Finally, look at the section between 3.63 and 3.64.

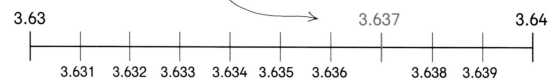

These show thousandths.

Make 3 number lines for each of these decimal numbers:

1. 5.125

2. 16.581

3. 23.332

4. 50.509

5. Choose 2 more decimal numbers of your own, and make number lines to explain them to a friend.

What is in between?

On a number line, the numbers between
4.366 and 4.371 are:

4.367, 4.368, 4.369, 4.370

4.366   4.367   4.368   4.369   4.370   4.371

Write the numbers between these pairs of decimals. Draw a
number line if it helps.

1. 1.752 and 1.757

2. 3.686 and 3.691

3. 10.250 and 10.258

4. 7.915 and 7.920

5. 25.46 and 25.464

6. 18.358 and 18.363

7. 2.997 and 3.003

8. 15.995 and 16

9. A decimal number is rounded from 3 decimal places
    to 2 decimal places. The rounded number is 5.42.
    Write all the possible numbers it could have been.

Missing decimal numbers

The number lines below have some values missing.
Copy each number line and fill in the missing numbers.

1.

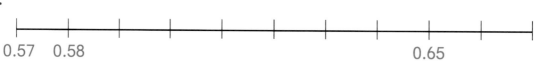

3.5   4.1

2.

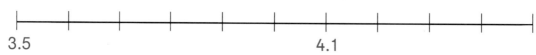

0.57   0.58   0.65

3.

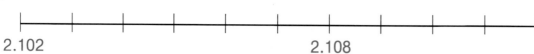

2.102   2.108

4.

9.96

5.

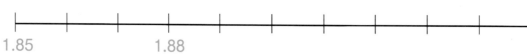

1.85   1.88

6.

15.5   15.6

7. Make a number line with missing decimals for a friend to try.

Making use of decimals

This drawing shows part of a stopwatch.

The watch measures time to a hundredth of a second.

The letter A shows 0.10 of a second.

1. What timings are shown by the other letters?

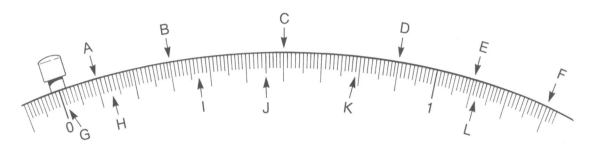

For an engine to work properly, the spark plug gap must be set between 0.84 mm and 0.97 mm.

Say whether these gaps are alright to make the engine work.

2. 0.848 mm   3. 0.876 mm

4. 0.837 mm   5. 0.951 mm

6. 0.98 mm   7. 0.972 mm

8. Use tracing paper to copy the circle. Join the points in decreasing order. Connect the last point and the first point to complete the design.

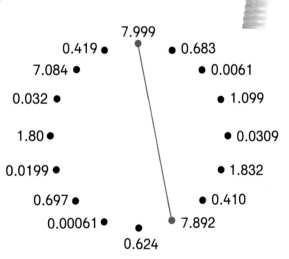

7.999

0.419 ●　　● 0.683

7.084 ●　　　● 0.0061

0.032 ●　　　　● 1.099

1.80 ●　　　　● 0.0309

0.0199 ●　　　　● 1.832

0.697 ●　　　● 0.410

0.00061 ●　　● 7.892

● 0.624

A classroom plan

Here is a classroom plan for 30 children.

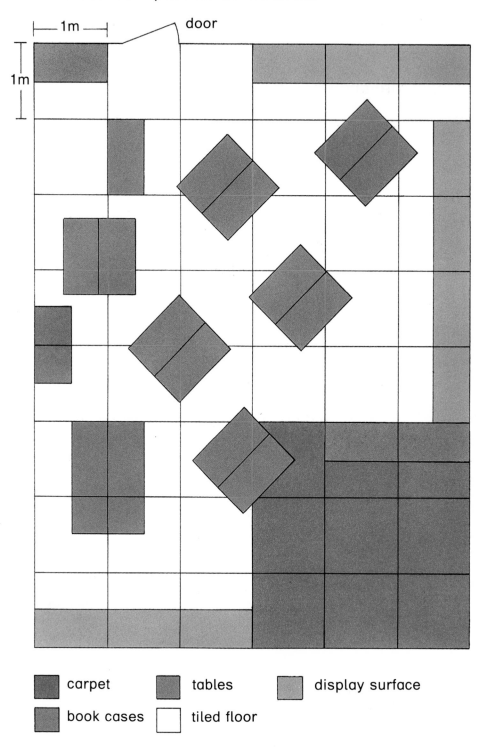

Fractions of the classroom

Use the plan on page 94 to answer these questions.

1. What is the total floor area of the classroom?

What fraction of the floor is:

2. carpeted?

3. covered by tables?

4. taken up by display areas?

5. covered in bookcases?

6. Make a plan of your classroom and show how the floor area is used. Write all the items as approximate fractions of the total area.

Fraction additions and subtractions

 and add together to make

$$\frac{1}{2} \quad + \quad \frac{1}{2} \quad = \quad 1$$

Use these pictures to help you work out the answers to these fraction additions:

1.

$$\frac{3}{4} + \frac{1}{4} =$$

2.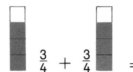

$$\frac{3}{4} + \frac{3}{4} =$$

3.

$$\frac{1}{3} \quad + \quad \frac{1}{3} \quad =$$

4.

$$\frac{1}{5} \quad + \quad \frac{2}{5} \quad =$$

5. $\frac{1}{3} + \frac{2}{3} =$ **6.** $\frac{1}{5} + \frac{1}{5} =$ **7.** $1\frac{1}{4} + \frac{1}{4} =$ **8.** $1\frac{2}{3} + \frac{2}{3} =$

Now try subtraction.

 take away leaves

$$\frac{2}{3} \quad - \quad \frac{1}{3} \quad = \quad \frac{1}{3}$$

Work out the answers to these fraction subtractions.

9.

$$\frac{3}{4} \quad - \quad \frac{1}{4} \quad =$$

10.

$$\frac{3}{5} \quad - \quad \frac{2}{5} \quad =$$

11.

$$\frac{5}{6} \quad - \quad \frac{1}{6} \quad =$$

12.

$$\frac{1}{3} \quad - \quad \frac{1}{3} \quad =$$

13. $\frac{4}{5} - \frac{2}{5} =$ **14.** $1\frac{1}{3} - \frac{2}{3} =$ **15.** $1\frac{1}{6} - \frac{5}{6} =$ **16.** $1\frac{1}{4} - \frac{3}{4} =$

Adding and subtracting different fractions

Remember: the bottom number of a fraction is the denominator.

The denominator tells you what sort of fraction it is.

The denominator of $\frac{1}{3}$ or $\frac{2}{3}$ is 3.

The denominator of $\frac{1}{4}$ or $\frac{3}{4}$ is 4.

When you add or subtract fractions with different denominators you need to convert them. One way to do this is to use towers of cubes. For example:

$\frac{1}{4} + \frac{1}{3} = ?$

$\frac{3}{12} + \frac{4}{12} = \frac{7}{12}$

Use towers of 12 cubes (12ths)

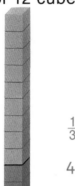

$\frac{1}{4}$ of 12 is

3 cubes $\frac{3}{12}$

$\frac{1}{3}$ of 12 is

4 cubes $\frac{4}{12}$

Use towers of 12 cubes to work these out:

1. $\frac{1}{4} + \frac{1}{6}$ 2. $\frac{1}{3} - \frac{1}{4}$

3. $\frac{2}{3} + \frac{1}{4}$ 4. $\frac{2}{3} - \frac{1}{2}$

Towers of 10 cubes might help with these:

5. $\frac{7}{10} + \frac{1}{5}$ 6. $\frac{3}{5} - \frac{3}{10}$

7. $\frac{1}{2} - \frac{1}{10}$ 8. $\frac{3}{10} + \frac{2}{5}$

Now try these:

9. $\frac{1}{4} - \frac{1}{5}$ 10. $\frac{1}{3} + \frac{2}{5}$

Using ratios in measuring

To make this orange drink taste right you need to mix it in the correct ratio:

water	to	orange
1000	:	250

The ratio can be made simpler by halving:

500 : 125

then ÷ 5

100 : 25

then ÷ 25

The simplest way of expressing the ratio of water to orange is 4 : 1.

This is very useful, because you may not want to make 1000 ml (a whole litre), but just 1 glass. Other liquids have to be mixed correctly.

Write these as ratios, in their simplest form:

1. 1 litre to 100 ml

2. 1 litre to 500 ml

3. 1 litre to 25 ml

4. 1 litre to 50 ml

We can use ratios with other kinds of measurements. Write these as ratios in their simplest form:

5. 1 m to 10 cm

6. 1 min to 15 sec

7. 3 kg to 60 g

8. £1 to 5p

9. 4 cm to 5 mm

10. 2 km to 400 m

Mixing colours

If 4 ml of red paint, 8 ml of blue paint and 6 ml of white paint are mixed together they make 18 ml of mauve paint.

If you want to make more (or less) mauve paint, but not change the shade of mauve, you need to keep the ratios exactly the same.

Copy and complete this chart for making different quantities of mauve paint.

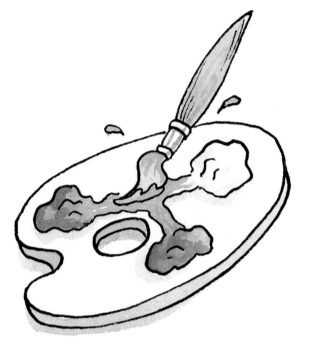

1.

red (ml)	4	2	6		14				12
blue (ml)	8	4		16				32	
white (ml)	6		9			30			
quantity of mauve (ml)	18						45		

2. What do you notice about the numbers in the bottom row?

Ratios are useful in all sorts of mixtures, including recipes.

Either:

Write out your favourite school recipe and change it to make 2 or 3 times as much.

or

Mix your own colour of paint and make a chart for making different quantities.

You could use brushfuls of paint instead of ml.

How could you continue?

The number sequence 1, 2, 3 could be developed
into a pattern in several different ways. For example,

1, 2, 3, 4, 5, 6 ...,

1, 2, 3, 1, 2, 3, 1, 2 ...

or 1, 2, 3, 2, 1, 2, 3 ...

1. Find 2 more ways to continue the sequence 1 2 3 ...

Find 3 different ways to continue each of these
sequences to make a pattern.

2. 1, 4   3. 3, 6

4. −4, −2   5. 10, 8

Explain how the numbers are changing in each of
these sequences.

6. 2 4 8 16 32 64 128

7. 44 41 38 35 32 29 26

8. 2 3 5 9 17 33 65

9. Make up some starting points of your own for a
   friend to try.

Find the function

This function machine multiplies every number
put into it by 2, then adds 1.

1. What sequence do you get if you carry on putting
   the counting numbers (1, 2, 3 ...) through the machine?

Now put the counting numbers through these function
machines.

2. +4 ÷ 2   3. −2 + 1   4. +5 x 3

If we keep putting numbers back into a function
machine we can produce a sequence or chain.

1 → 3 → 7 → 15

Suggest the function machines that could have
produced these chains:

5. 1, 5, 17, 53   6. 2, 3, 5, 9

   Make a number chain for a friend to work out.

Areas of parallelograms...

Remember: the area of a parallelogram can be found by multiplying the base length by the height.

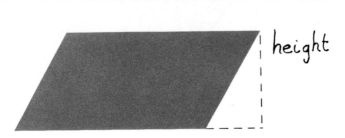

height

base

Find the areas of these shapes.

1.

2.

3.

4.

... and triangles

Remember: the area of a triangle is $\frac{1}{2}$ (base x height).

Find the areas of these shapes.

1.

2.

3.

4.

5.

6.

Volumes of prisms

Remember: a prism is a solid with 2 congruent parallel faces.

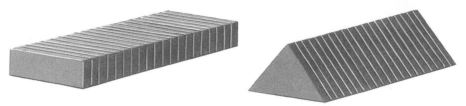

The volume of a prism may be found by multiplying
the area of its end faces by its length.

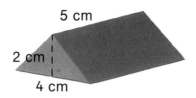

5 cm

2 cm

4 cm

Face area $= \frac{1}{2}(4 \times 2) = 4 \text{ cm}^2$

Volume $= 4 \times 5 = 20 \text{ cm}^3$

What is the volume of these prisms?

1.

1 cm

3 cm   6 cm

2.

2 cm

2 cm   5 cm

How long are these prisms?

3.

3 cm

3 cm

Volume
$= 36 \text{ cm}^2$

4.

5 cm

4 cm

Volume =
50 cm^2

How high are these prisms?

5.

Volume
$= 72 \text{ cm}^3$

6 cm   6 cm

6.

Volume
$= 15 \text{ cm}^3$

2 cm   3 cm

Volumes and surface areas

2 cm

3 cm

5 cm

This cuboid has 2 faces with area 6 cm^2

2 faces with area 10 cm^2

2 faces with area 15 cm^2

Its total surface area is 62 cm^2.

Its volume = 30 cm^3.

1. What is the surface area of this square prism?

2. What is its volume?

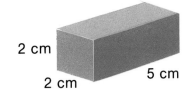

2 cm

2 cm

5 cm

3. What is the surface area of this triangular prism?

5 cm

4 cm

6 cm

8 cm

4. What is its volume?

5. Four different cuboids each have a volume of 12 cm^3.
   What are their surface areas?

All sorts of parallelograms

Remember: a parallelogram has 2 pairs of parallel sides.
Here are some parallelograms made on a
4 x 4 geoboard.

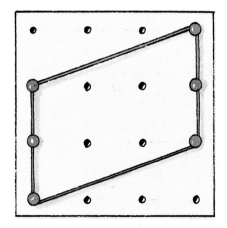

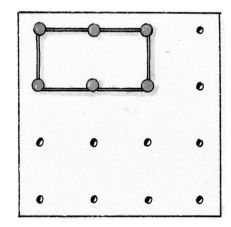

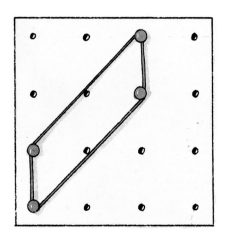

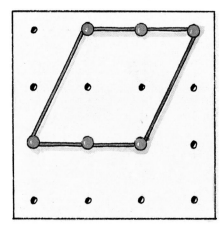

1. Make some more parallelograms on a
    4 x 4 geoboard. Draw them on square or
    spotty paper.

2. Make all the parallelograms you can on a
    3 x 3 geoboard. Draw them on square or
    spotty paper.

More parallelograms

1. Here is a way to draw several parallelograms quickly.

    Draw straight lines on either side of a ruler.
    Move the ruler down a line, draw another line, and so
    on. Now turn the ruler so that it crosses the first set of
    lines and do the same.
    Make a parallelogram pattern. What is special about
    the parallelograms you have drawn?

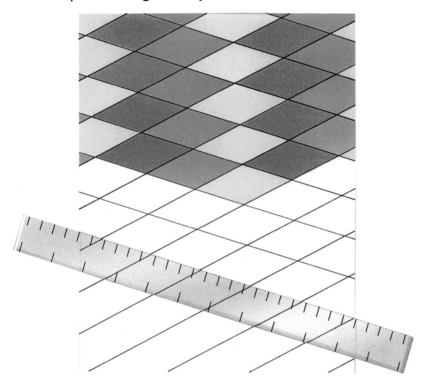

2. Use isometric (triangular) paper to
    draw a variety of parallelograms
    and rhombuses.
    Measure the angles inside your
    shapes. What do you notice?

Nodes, branches and regions

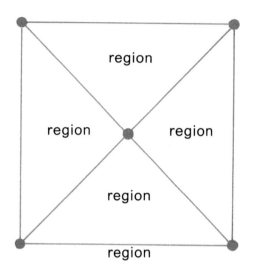

region

region   region

region

region

This is an example of a network. It has 5 nodes. These are points on the network.

It has 8 branches. These are the lines connecting the nodes.

Where branches and nodes join up to enclose spaces they make regions. The outside of the network is also a region, so this network has 5 regions.

Now look at this network.

    It has 4 nodes.

    It has 8 branches.

    It has 6 regions.

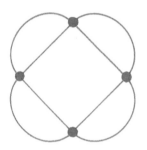

Count the nodes, branches and regions for each of these networks.

1.

2.

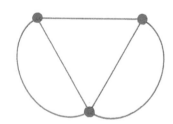

3.

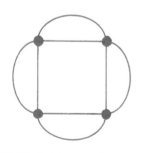

4.

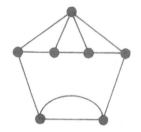

More nodes, branches and regions

a.
b.
c.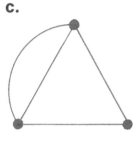

Each network has 3 nodes, but a different
number of branches and regions. This is shown
in the table.

	nodes	regions	branches
a	3	5	6
b	3	4	5
c	3	3	4

Draw some networks with 4 nodes and some
networks with 5 nodes.
Continue the table.
What is the connection between the number
of nodes, regions and branches?

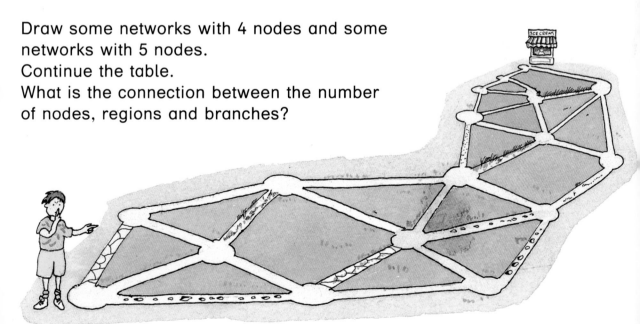

Moving around networks

If you can move right around a network without going over any branch more than once, the network is called traversable.

Which of these networks is traversable?

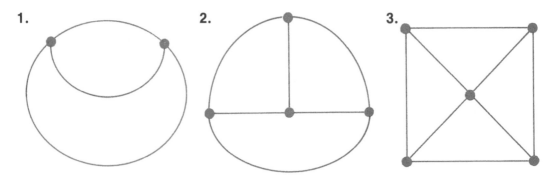

1.   2.   3.

A node with an odd number of branches coming from it is called an odd node.
A node with an even number of branches is an even node.

For each of these networks count the number of odd nodes, and say whether the network is traversable.

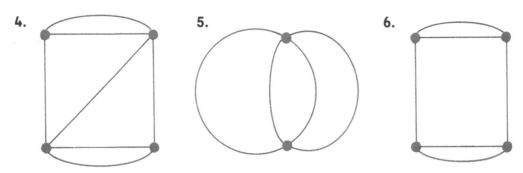

4.   5.   6.

Draw some more networks.
Investigate the connection between traversability and the number of odd nodes.

Crossing bridges

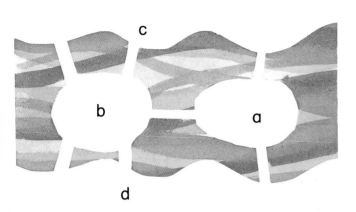

This is a famous puzzle called the Königsberg Bridge Problem. Can you travel over each bridge once and once only?

By drawing the map of Königsberg as a network the problem becomes:

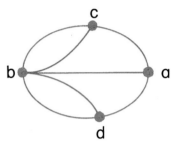

1. Is this network traversable?

    Each branch represents one of the bridges.

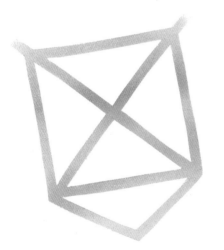

A paper-round covers these streets.

2. Draw it as a network with the streets as branches and the intersections as nodes.

3. Is it traversable?

4. Draw a street plan that is traversable and another that is not.

Pairs of angles

Two angles that add up to 90° are complementary angles.

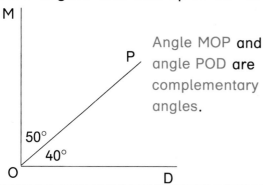

Angle MOP and angle POD are complementary angles.

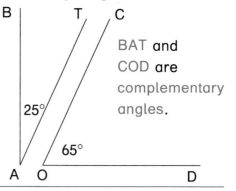

BAT and COD are complementary angles.

When 2 lines intersect, the opposite angles are equal.

MAT and CAB are opposite angles.

MAT = CAB = 70°

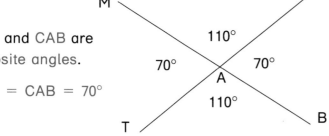

MAC and TAB are opposite angles.

MAC = TAB = 110°

Two angles that add up to 180° are supplementary angles.

FAT and FAN are supplementary angles.

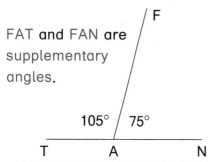

TAP and NOW are supplementary angles.

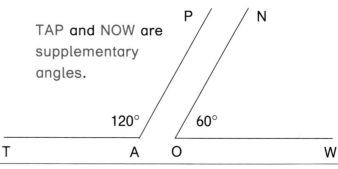

Calculate the angle marked x°.

1.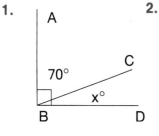

2.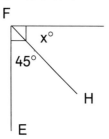

3.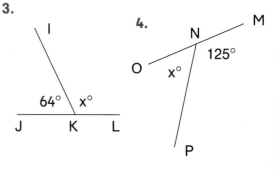

4.

Calculating angles

Are these pairs of angles complementary, supplementary or opposite angles?

1.

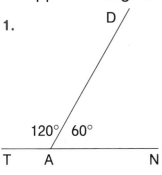

120° 60°

T   A   N

2.

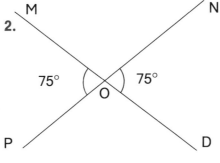

M   N

75°   75°

O

P   D

3.

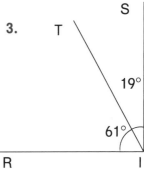

S

T

19°

61°

R   I

Calculate the unknown angles x and y.

4.

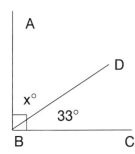

A

x°

33°

B   C

5.

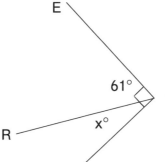

E

61°   F

R   x°

G

6.

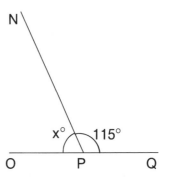

N

x°   115°

O   P   Q

7.

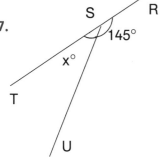

S   R

145°

x°

T

U

8.

A

y°

94°   x°

B

C   D

E

9.

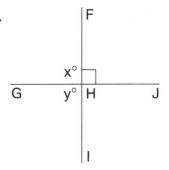

F

x°

G   y°   H   J

I

What are the complementary angles of these?

10. 30°   **11.** 65°   **12.** 42°   **13.** 8°

What are the supplementary angles of these?

14. 30°   **15.** 145°   **16.** 98°   **17.** 159°

Reading pie charts

This pie chart was drawn to show how 36 children came to school.

What fraction:

1. came by car?

2. walked?

3. came by bus?

How many:

4. came by car?

5. walked?

6. came by bus?

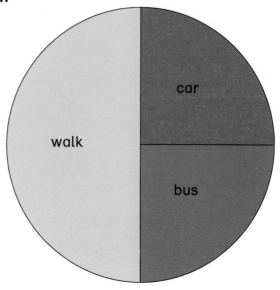

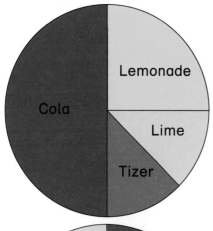

These pie charts show the results of a survey of 40 children's favourite fast foods and drinks.

What fraction of children preferred:

7. Tizer?

8. Lemonade?

How many children preferred:

9. Lime?

10. Cola?

Approximately what percentage preferred:

11. Burgers?

12. Fried Chicken?

13. Fish and Chips?

Draw a pie chart

To draw a pie chart, start with a circle. Then divide the circle into the number of sectors you need. This one has been divided into 8. You can use it to show halves, quarters and eighths.

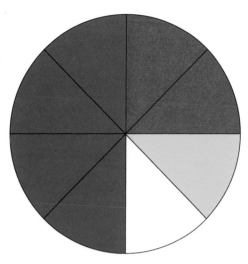

You could use a protractor to divide the circle into sectors.

Draw pie charts to show these pieces of information:

1. In a traffic survey, half the vehicles seen were cars, one quarter were lorries, one eighth were buses, one eighth were bicycles.

2. Out of 50 children,
   10 wore red tops,
   20 wore blue tops and
   20 wore yellow tops.

3. In a pets survey,
   40% owned dogs,
   20% owned cats,
   20% kept birds and
   20% had fish.

There is more about pie charts on the next page.

Jenny's day

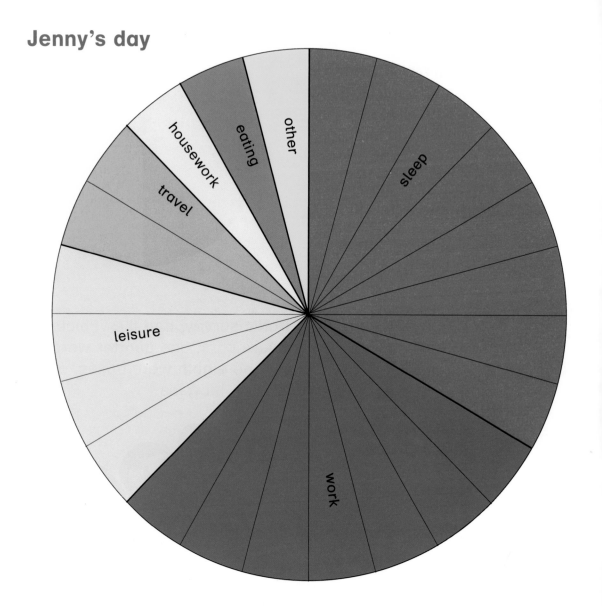

This pie chart shows how Jenny spends a typical day.

1. Write down how many hours she spends on each activity.

2. What kinds of activities might come under 'other'?

3. Make a pie chart of your own day.

Representing and interpreting data   Unit 2   Interpreting a pie chart

Unfair dice and spinners

Make this unfair spinner.

> You will need a circle of card coloured as shown.
> Attach a card arrow to the centre with a paper fastener or drawing pin so it spins freely.

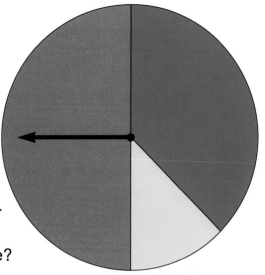

1. Spin the spinner 50 or 60 times. Keep a tally of the colours. Make a pie chart of your results. Compare it with the spinner itself. What do you notice?

2. Try a similar experiment with a cube.
   Colour 1 face red, 2 faces yellow, and 3 faces blue.
   Roll it several times.
   Keep a record of the colours and make a pie chart.

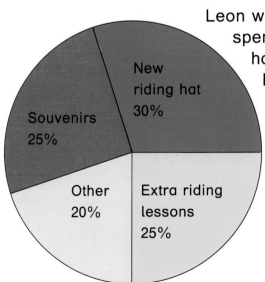

Leon went on a riding holiday. He took £50 spending money. This pie chart shows how he spent it.

How much money did he spend on each of these:

3. new riding hat?

4. souvenirs?

5. extra riding lessons?

6. other things?

British mammals

These 2 pages show a set of children's data cards about British mammals. The information is not very well organised. For example, some of the measurements are in inches and some are in cm. The children have used many different words to describe what the mammals eat.

1. Look carefully at the information on the cards and plan a clear database to hold all the information. If possible put your database on to a computer.

2. Enter all the information from the cards into your database.
   You may wish to add more information about the mammals.
   You may wish to add more mammals.

Otter
The otter eats fish.
It has 2 or 3 cubs.
It is 105 cm from nose to tail.

Dormouse
Diet: herbivore
Litter: 4
Length: 13.75 cm

Pine Marten
The pine marten is carnivorous.
Including its tail it is 82.5 cm long.
It has between 3 and 5 babies.

Stoat
Length: 40 cm
Young: 5 or more
Diet: carnivorous

Weasel
Eats rabbits and hares.
Measures 10 inches.
Has five or six babies.

Red Squirrel
The red squirrel feeds on nuts and berries. Although it tucks its tail up behind it, its total length is 42 to 43 cm long. The squirrel has between two and four kittens, which live in its drey.

Badger
The badger is 30 inches long.
It eats small mammals, insects, roots and fruits.
The female has 3 or 4 young.

Hare
length, 25 inches
Diet, grass, clover, young corn
Young, 2 to 5

Water vole
This is the biggest vole at 30 cm.
It lives near water. It can swim.
It lives on plants, including some farm vegetables. It has five young.

Harvest Mouse
Body: 2.5 inches
Tail: 2 inches
Even though the harvest mouse is the smallest mouse in Britain, it has as many as nine young.
It eats only corn and seeds.

Rabbit
Rabbits are common herbivores which breed very rapidly, having up to eight young in every litter. The average full grown rabbit is 50 centimetres long.

Hedgehog
Although the hedgehog eats mainly worms and insects, it also likes fruit and bread and milk as well as eggs.
When it is unrolled it is 25 cm long. The average litter is four.

Shrews
Shrews are our smallest mammals.
The common is only 4 inches long, and the pigmy is only 7 cm. They both have up to 7 young and are carnivorous.
They eat insects like beetles, and worms.

Wild Cat
The wild cat eats small birds and mammals. It is about 90 cm long and has between 2 and 5 kittens.

Fox
Length: 40 inches
Litter size: up to 7 cubs
Food: mainly meat, but will eat scraps of household waste.

Brown rat
Omnivorous
42.15 cm including tail
14 young

The Amazing Bat
There are many varieties of bat native to Britain. They vary in size from the Greater Horseshoe Bat, with a wingspan of 30 cm and a body of 4 inches to the Pipistrel which is only 5 cm long with a 6 inch wingspan.
They are flying predators, the larger varieties catch moths and flying beetles on the wing. The smaller varieties prey mainly on gnats and small flies.
They are nocturnal. Females carry a single offspring on their chests even when hunting. They use ultra-sonic frequencies for locating prey and direction finding.

Moles
It is amazing to think that a tiny creature less than 10 inches long can make tunnels hundreds, and even thousands, of feet long. It does this mainly to find its favourite food, worms. In doing this, it often damages roots. The tunnels also contain the mole's nest which often has five young in it.

Let's find out – playgrounds

These 2 pages should give you some ideas about things you can investigate to do with the playground.

Look at these 2 photographs. Compare the 2 playgrounds. List similarities and differences. Compare them with your own playground.

Find out what people think of your playground.
Don't forget to include younger children.

You will need to consider:

exactly what question you want answered

how many people to ask

which people to ask

how to collect their views

how to summarise their views.

Here are some ideas for questions.

There is nothing to do
in the playground.

The playground is too crowded.

What markings are needed
on the playground?

Have we got enough furniture
in the playground, such as
litter bins and seats?

Let's find out – school traffic

These pages should give you some ideas about things you can investigate to do with people moving around your school.

Choose any one you are really interested in.
You will need to decide:

Is there a problem to investigate?

Whose problem is it?

What data will make the situation clearer?

How can you present your findings?

What are the possible solutions?

Start with your classroom.
How do people move around it?

One way to find out might be to make a sketch plan.
Watch people moving around the classroom and draw lines on the plan to show their routes.

This survey could be done in another part of the school.
Look for wear and tear on carpets and tiles.

Handling data contexts   Unit 4   Collecting, processing, representing and interpreting data in the context of school traffic

These are other interesting areas to research.
You should be able to suggest improvements
from your findings.

Are there any parts of the
school which become
overcrowded at certain times of
the day? Try to find out why this
happens and if there is anything
you can do about it.

Are there any parts of the
school or classroom which are
over used or under used? What
kinds of alterations would you
make?

Can anybody get into your
school? What about people in
wheelchairs or with walking
sticks? Alternatively, is it easy
for burglars or vandals to get
in?

If there was a fire, how would
you get out? It is always wise to
have at least 2 possible escape
routes. Try to design a network
which would allow you to
escape from any part of the
school.

Predict and test ...

If you throw a drawing pin into the air, it could
land in 3 possible ways:

> on its back
>
> on its point
>
> on its point and its edge

1. Predict which of these landings you think
    will happen most often. Say why.

2. Which do you think will happen least often?
    Say why.

3. Now experiment by dropping a drawing pin
    50 times. Say whether the experiment
    confirmed your predictions.

Use 2 real coins.

If you flip them in the air they could land showing 2 heads.

4. What other ways could they land?

5. Which do you think is most likely? Why?

6. Try tossing 2 coins 50 times.
    Record the results.
    Say whether your prediction was right.

...and predict again

Use 3 real coins.

If you flip them in the air they could land showing 3 heads.

1. What other ways could they land?

2. Which do you think is more likely, 3 heads
   or 2 heads and a tail?
   Say why.

3. Which do you think is more likely, 2 heads and a tail
   or 2 tails and a head?
   Say why.

4. Toss 3 coins 50 times. Record the results.
   Say whether the results agree with your predictions.
   If they do not, try and explain why.

Glossary

arrowhead A quadrilateral with two pairs of adjacent sides equal and a reflex angle.

axes The lines, usually perpendicular, which form the reference points in a co-ordinate system.

bearing A direction expressed as the angle, measured clockwise, from north.

co-ordinates Ordered pairs used to show position on a grid, map or graph.

data Pieces of information, for example, the heights of each member of the class.

database An organised collection of data, often kept on a computer.

denominator The bottom part of a fraction numeral, for example the 4 in $\frac{3}{4}$.

digital root The sum of the digits of a number.

factor A factor of a number is any number that will divide into it exactly.

factorise Express a number as the product of its factors. For example, 6 = 2 x 3.

formula A function expressing the relationship between two or more measures, for example, AREA = LENGTH x BREADTH.

frequency The number of times a particular outcome occurs when data is being counted.

function A combination of operations and numbers describing something done to a number. For example, x 3 or + 2 x 4.

kite A quadrilateral with two pairs of adjacent sides equal.

mean   A type of average. The mean of a set of data is found by adding the data and dividing the result by the number of data.

median   The middle element of an ordered set of data.

mode   The value which appears most often in a set of data. The mode of 6, 5, 6, 2, 6, is 6.

numerator   The top part of fraction numeral, for example, the 3 in $\frac{3}{4}$.

ordered pair   Two numbers whose order of writing is significant. For example: the x and y co-ordinates on a graph.

parallelogram   Any quadrilateral in which both pairs of opposite sides are parallel.

pi (π)   A special number approximately equal to 3.14. It is the ratio of the circumference of a circle to its diameter.

pie chart   A circle divided into sectors to represent fractions or percentages of a whole.

plane of symmetry   An imaginary slice through a solid shape dividing it into two symmetrical halves.

prime factor   A prime number that is a factor of another number. 3 and 2 are prime factors of 12.

prime number   A number whose only factors are 1 and itself.

prism   A solid shape whose end faces are congruent and parallel. The other faces are rectangles.

quadrant   One of four separate regions of a graph separated by the x and y axes.

quadrilateral   Any four-sided polygon.

ratio   A way of comparing the size of one number or measure with another. It is found by dividing one of the numbers into the other.

reciprocal   The reciprocal of a number is 1 divided by that number.

rhombus Any parallelogram whose sides are all the same length.

rotational symmetry A shape or pattern has rotational symmetry if it fits back into its 'frame' before it has made a full turn.

trapezium A quadrilateral with one pair of opposite sides parallel.

Keeping Fit

By Paul Bennett

MSC

ress

First published in Great Britain in 1997 by
 Belitha Press Limited
London House, Great Eastern Wharf
Parkgate Road, London SW11 4NQ

Reprinted 1998

Editor: Veronica Ross
Series designer: Hayley Cove
Photographer: Claire Paxton
Illustrator: Cilla Eurich
Picture researcher: Diana Morris
Consultant: Elizabeth Atkinson

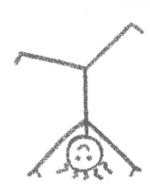

ISBN 1 85561 589 4 (hardback)
ISBN 1 85561 779 X (paperback)

Printed in Hong Kong

Photo credits
Bubbles Photo Library: 16. Sally and Michael
Greenhill: 21, 26. Zefa-Stockmarket: 17
Michael Heron, 26 Jost L. Pelaez.

Thanks to models Topel, Jodie, Ricky, Bianca,
Meera, Stephen, Fiona.

Words in **bold** are explained in the list of useful
words on pages 30 and 31.